THE MONEY COACH

Your Game Plan for
Growth, Tax Relief,
and Security

RILEY MOYNES
with
Jack P. Friedman, Ph.D., CPA

7896590

First edition for the United States published by Barron's
Educational Series, Inc., 1998.

Copyright © 1996 by Addison-Wesley Publishers Ltd. and Ashlar
House Inc.

All inquiries should be addressed to:
Barron's Educational Series, Inc.
250 Wireless Boulevard
Hauppauge, New York 11788
http://www.barronseduc.com

International Standard Book No. 0-7641-0579-5

Library of Congress Catalog Card No. 97-31312

Library of Congress Cataloging-in-Publication Data

Moynes, Riley E., 1944–
     The money coach : your game plan for growth, tax relief, and
security / Riley Moynes.—1st ed. for the U.S.
         p.   cm.
     ISBN 0-7641-0579-5
     1. Finance, Personal—United States.   2. Investments—United
States.   I. Title.
HG179.M69   1998
332.024'01—dc21   97-31312
                                                                          CIP

Printed in the United States of America

9 8 7 6 5 4 3 2 1

CONTENTS

P R E F A C E

When *The Money Coach* was first published in Canada in November 1992, I had no idea how it would be received. American authors Andrew Tobias and Sylvia Porter were widely read, but, with the exception of David Chilton's *The Wealthy Barber*, no Canadian financial book had really captured the imagination of the public at large. I was convinced that with its easy-to-read style and dazzling graphics in full "Technicolor," *The Money Coach* would be very different from all the others, and that was part of our intent. But how would it be received by the public?

Five years later we are gratified at the enormous, positive response we have received. The book was selected by the Book-of-the-Month Club. Individuals and companies within the financial industry have viewed it as an ideal means of reinforcing some key concepts with their clients—and have bought the book by the hundreds and thousands. And individual Canadians, more and more interested in the whole area of investments, tax savings, and retirement planning, have embraced *The Money Coach*, sometimes literally.

With each revision and expansion, we have attempted to stick to the basics, to make the information as fresh and current as possible, and to introduce new concepts, topics, and graphics. Often, new concepts and graphics were field-tested during seminars at which I was invited to speak across the country.

With this American edition, we begin a new chapter in the book's history. Every portion of the book has been carefully reviewed and revised to make it applicable to American readers. Figures and data have been updated to make the book as current as possible. It is our hope that *The Money Coach* will be as useful and indispensable for Americans as it has become for Canadians.

The Money Coach is also becoming increasingly research-driven. There is a growing body of research, part of which we are creating, indicating that there are strategies and approaches to investment that clearly work better than others. While past editions have referred to pertinent research, this edition and future ones will HIGHLIGHT it. As always, we must remember that, contrary to public opinion, knowledge itself is not power. Applied knowledge is powerful; so we must use the research to benefit from it.

As we said in the original edition: "This book has been written to share with you the simple, commonsense ideas and principles that, if acted upon, will, over a period of time, create the assets that can help ensure the secure, worry-free retirement years we all dream of—but that very few of us achieve.

"Read on, learn, enjoy, and act! You'll be glad you did."

Riley E. Moynes

Jack P. Friedman

(American edition)

I N T R O D U C T I O N

Are you winning the money "game"?

Do you know that you're playing the money game?

Like it or not, we are all forced to play this game from the time we begin to earn money through the rest of our lives. Taxes must be paid, bills must be paid, and loans must be paid. Money must be allocated for food, rent or mortgage, telephone, car payments, credit cards, insurance, new clothes for the kids, and so on. Savings are necessary for that trip, for schooling, for retirement. The list seems endless.

How do you learn to play the money game successfully? The sad truth is that some people never do. Those who succeed often do so in a hit-or-miss fashion, more through good luck than good management. Some of us learn from parents or others, although most of what they learned was through sometimes bitter experience.

Unfortunately, very little formal attention is given to the topic in our schools. The attitude seems to be either that it's something that comes naturally (like walking and talking), or that it's not all that important. Both assumptions are very, very wrong!

Sometimes we turn to "professionals" for help, and they can be helpful in certain ways. Accountants have detailed knowledge of Internal Revenue Codes, and, while that is important to the rules of the financial game, it's by no means the only part. Lawyers who specialize in tax law can be helpful in certain areas, but beyond that may have no particular financial expertise. A bank manager may be helpful when it comes to providing a needed mortgage or loan, or in telling you what the current CD or passbook savings account rates are, but there's a lot more to the game than that.

Then there's the IRS. Again, someone there may be able to help you, although you may be given four different answers to the same tax-related question by four different IRS employees!

And again, their expertise is limited to aspects and interpretations of the Internal Revenue Code. Even so, Tax Court is the ultimate referee in the money game.

So to whom do you turn to help you play the game effectively and successfully? You need a money coach. That's why this book was written: to help you understand the financial "big picture," and to help you develop the skills and knowledge necessary to compete successfully in the financial game. You're forced to play the game, so you might as well get all the help you can to play it well!

But good coaching does not come exclusively from a book. After you read this one, I urge you to find your own money coach who will continue to work with you. An effective coach will keep you up to date on the continual changes to the rules of the game. Your money coach will help you to further develop the financial skills you'll learn from this book by practicing them with you and giving feedback on how well you're using them.

Some people call them financial advisors or planners, investment consultants, insurance agents, or stockbrokers. I call them "money coaches." I urge you to find one with whom you're comfortable, in whom you have confidence, and who provides you with outstanding service. It can be a very satisfying, productive, and successful relationship, as well as a positive learning experience.

And good luck as you play the financial game. I am confident that *The Money Coach* will help you play it successfully. You may even turn out to be a star in the game!

CHAPTER 1

THE GAME PLAN

t's not how much money you make that's important, it's how much you keep.

Quite simply, this book is about accumulating wealth so that you can become "financially free." To me, you are financially free when you can do what you want, where you want, when you want, and with whom you want. For some, that will permit travel and the acquisition of things; for others, it will allow charitable donations and assistance to family and friends.

Unfortunately, three major obstacles prevent us from keeping as much as we'd like—and as much as we deserve.

These three obstacles are:

- taxes
- inflation
- no plan

TAXES

In theory, taxes are imposed by governments at all levels and paid by Americans in order to fund services that are required or desired by the people. These include such diverse services as national defense, transportation, highway construction, mail delivery, garbage pickup, and many others.

Unfortunately, for a variety of reasons including government mismanagement, Americans are now among the most heavily taxed people in the world. One research group, The Tax Foundation in Washington, D.C., calculates that while in 1956 less than 28% of the income of the average American family was paid in taxes of all kinds, the figure had increased to more than 38% for a two-income family in 1996.

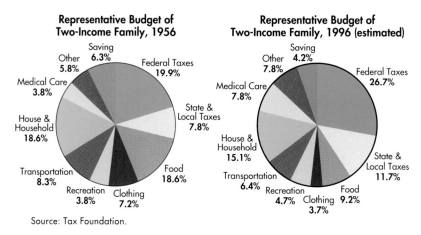

Representative Budget of Two-Income Family, 1956

Saving 6.3%
Other 5.8%
Federal Taxes 19.9%
Medical Care 3.8%
State & Local Taxes 7.8%
House & Household 18.6%
Transportation 8.3%
Food 18.6%
Recreation 3.8%
Clothing 7.2%

Representative Budget of Two-Income Family, 1996 (estimated)

Saving 4.2%
Other 7.8%
Federal Taxes 26.7%
Medical Care 7.8%
House & Household 15.1%
State & Local Taxes 11.7%
Transportation 6.4%
Recreation 4.7%
Clothing 3.7%
Food 9.2%

Source: Tax Foundation.

The trend appears to be inevitable: an ever-increasing amount of personal income consumed by taxes.

Unfortunately, most Americans seem to be resigned to this sorry situation. You'll learn by reading on, however, that there are several ways of reducing your tax burden and keeping more of your own money.

Think of paying taxes as a game. You probably wouldn't decide to play a game before you knew the rules—you'd be afraid of embarrassing yourself publicly—and you know that you can't play any game effectively without knowing the rules that apply. Your coach or someone teaches you the rules, and you can then play more effectively.

It's the same with taxes, except that we are all forced to play the tax game —we have no choice. All the rules apply, but we don't know them well. Therefore, we play the tax game poorly. And when was the last time your friendly Internal Revenue Service representative called to suggest tax reduction strategies or to clarify the tax rules for you? The IRS is not the coach—it's the umpire. You must either get a money coach (a financial advisor, a tax lawyer, an accountant, a trusted friend) or teach yourself. Most of us do neither. Small wonder we don't play the tax game well and therefore pay more in taxes than is necessary!

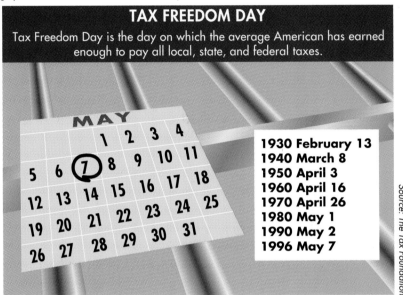

TAX FREEDOM DAY

Tax Freedom Day is the day on which the average American has earned enough to pay all local, state, and federal taxes.

MAY

1	2	3	4	
5	6	⑦ 8	9 10	11
12	13 14	15	16 17	18
19	20 21	22	23 24	25
26	27 28	29	30 31	

1930 February 13
1940 March 8
1950 April 3
1960 April 16
1970 April 26
1980 May 1
1990 May 2
1996 May 7

Source: The Tax Foundation

Tax freedom day, excluding federal deficits, was May 7 in 1996; it was February 13 in 1930.

INFLATION

While most people seem to be aware of taxes (though they may not know what to do about them), they seem to be unaware of the insidiousness of inflation. It truly is a silent, stalking enemy that assaults—and can even destroy—our financial health in the same way that cancer attacks and can ruin our physical health.

In simple terms, inflation eats into and reduces our buying power on an ongoing basis. Twenty years ago in 1977 it cost 13¢ to mail a first-class letter in the United States; in 1997 it costs 32¢! That's inflation! If this rate of inflation continues for the next twenty years, it will cost 79¢ to mail a first-class letter.

Inflation also devastates your investment returns. Over the last decade, inflation has virtually swallowed up or offset

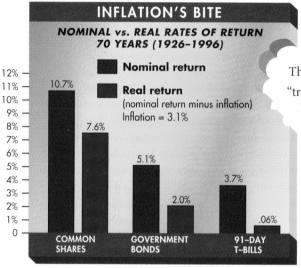

INFLATION'S BITE

**NOMINAL vs. REAL RATES OF RETURN
70 YEARS (1926–1996)**

■ Nominal return

■ Real return
(nominal return minus inflation)
Inflation = 3.1%

	COMMON SHARES	GOVERNMENT BONDS	91-DAY T-BILLS
Nominal return	10.7%	5.1%	3.7%
Real return	7.6%	2.0%	.06%

Source: Ibbotson Associates,
"Stocks, Bonds, Bills, and Inflation,"
Year-End Summary Report 1996.

Money Coach Rule

Always take inflation into account when calculating investment gains. It's the only way to get a true sense of the progress that has been achieved.

most wage increases that have been achieved by Americans.

The result: most people are "treading water" at best, and not getting ahead in real terms.

Inflation also hits hard at pensioners who do not have inflation protection as part of their plan. It cuts the purchasing power of a $40,000 pension in half to $20,000 in about 15 years (at an average inflation rate of 5%).

On the bright side, there is one good thing that can be said of inflation: It has allowed virtually every American homeowner to live in a more expensive neighborhood without moving!

NO PLAN

If you don't know where you are going, any road will do.   —*Chinese proverb*

Unfortunately, this quotation is true for the vast majority of Americans. Over 90% of us do nothing that could reasonably be called financial planning.

It's not that people plan to fail. Rather, they fail to plan.

Financial planning is essentially the proper handling of income and cash to meet your goals. A financial plan should be "one page simple" and generally should not include a monthly or weekly budget. I admire those who are careful budgeters and spend their money wisely. These people display an excellent sense of self-control. However, you don't need to be a compulsive budgeter or champion bargain hunter to build wealth. And, don't confuse the "big picture" of investing with the small details of everyday spending.

So far we have outlined the situation that many people find themselves in:

● They're paying large amounts in tax—likely more than necessary.

● They're being hurt by inflation without even realizing it.

● They don't know what they're trying to achieve and have no plan to achieve it.

Now let's look at what can and should be done to create a financial plan.

· COACH'S PLAYBOOK ·

How to build a financial plan

A financial plan should contain three simple parts:

Part 1. A snapshot of where you are financially, i.e., a statement of assets, obligations, and income.

Part 2. A statement or at least a sense of where you want to be in the short term (one year) and the longer term (three to five years), i.e., a goal or goals.

Part 3. A list of actions to be taken to get you from where you are to where you want to be.

Most people have no difficulty with Part 1 or 2 of their financial plan; Part 3 can be more difficult unless you know some of the strategies. That's what this book will help you learn. But you should also have some help from someone you trust in putting together a series of actions to be taken or decisions to be made; in other words, find yourself a money coach.

Ideally you won't depend too much on others to help you develop and implement your plan. Ultimately, we must all take responsibility for our own financial future. Fortunately, the basic principles to help you do that are really very simple. Not only can you learn them but you can also learn to apply them. That's where the fun and the results come in!

Here's what a simple financial plan looks like:

PART 1

GENERAL INFORMATION

YES	NO	
○	○	1. Do you have a current will?
○	○	2. Do you have a child/grandchild education fund?
○	○	3. Do you anticipate a significant inheritance?
○	○	4. Do you face any major life changes (marriage, job, move)?
○	○	5. Is your home owned jointly with your spouse?

6. What is your current income from all sources?

_____

7. What is the approximate rate of return on your current tax-sheltered retirement account?

_____

8. How much life insurance coverage do you have?

_____

9. How much income tax did you pay last year?

_____

10. How many years until your expected retirement?

_____

11. What is your expected retirement income?

_____

CURRENT NET WORTH

ASSETS		OBLIGATIONS	
Savings	_____	Mortgage principal	_____
Stocks, bonds, mutual funds	_____	Credit cards	_____
Home	_____	Loans	_____
Other property	_____	Support payments	_____
Autos	_____	Line of credit	_____
IRAs	_____	Other mortgages	_____
Vested retirement funds	_____	Other	_____
Other	_____	Total obligations	_____
Total assets	_____	**Net Worth**	_____
		(assets minus obligations)	

ASSESSMENT

What aspects of your current situation are you:

Most pleased about?

_____
_____
_____
_____
_____

Least pleased about?

_____
_____
_____
_____
_____

PART 2

What are your current financial priorities (e.g., buy new car, pay off mortgage, pay less tax, save for vacation, renovate, etc.)?

_____
_____
_____
_____

Where do you want to be financially in 5 to 10 years (e.g., have no mortgage, pay less tax, acquire an investment portfolio, prepare for retirement, start your own business.)?

_____
_____
_____
_____
_____

THE THREE GOALS OF FINANCIAL INDEPENDENCE

I'm convinced that if people patiently and consistently focused on the following simple financial goals, they would be well on the road to financial independence.

These goals will represent different priorities for different people depending on their age and circumstances. But, taken together, they represent a very powerful set of objectives.

We can achieve all three key objectives. But to do so, we must be prepared to make some decisions that do not always have guaranteed results. I'm convinced this is the preferred way to go.

These few pages have attempted to set the stage for later chapters and to put the more specific suggestions that follow in perspective.

We have identified your financial goals of growth, tax relief, and security. You know, at least in general terms, where you want to go. You're ready to examine the strategies and suggestions that lie ahead. You're ready to put your game plan into action.

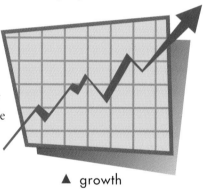

▲ growth

◄ tax relief

▼ security

CHAPTER 2

Get GROWING

A recent national poll found that three in four workers "worry that they won't have enough money to live comfortably in retirement." Your investments must grow for the amount to be adequate when you retire. A strong commitment to seek growth is vital for two main reasons:

1. To Avoid Being Limited Exclusively to Pension Income in Retirement

An astonishing statistic is that three out of five elderly Americans depend on Social Security benefits for three-quarters of their total retirement income! Some Americans are fortunate because they belong to a pension plan where they work. The typical person who retires with a pension receives 34% of his or her pre-retirement income from the pension. Combined with Social Security benefits, such a pension will typically replace

INCOME GAP AT RETIREMENT

$50,000 –
$40,000 –
$30,000 –
$20,000 –
$10,000 –
0 –

Pre-Retirement
Income

Old Age and Survivors
Insurance (Social Security)
after retirement

40–50%, or at most 70%, of pre-retirement income. Many hardworking people will live in retirement on as little as 25% of their former income, and that prospect is scary.

Fewer than half (47%) of all American wage and salary workers are enrolled in a tax-sheltered retirement program or company pension plan. The remaining 53% have no savings or investment program for retirement other than Social Security.

At most, benefits from Social Security replace only about one-third of your earnings. The maximum currently available from all government sources is less than $2,000 per month for a wage earner and spouse combined ($1,300 for a wage earner only).

The formula for determining future Social Security retirement benefits is complicated. To get a personalized statement of historical contributions and an estimate of benefits, call 1-800-722-1213. Ask for a *Request for Earnings and Benefit Estimate Statement.* If you're married, get two so your spouse can complete one also. The form(s) will arrive by mail within two weeks. Complete this simple form, return it to the Social Security Administration, and they will provide a detailed tabulation of amounts paid in, and an estimate of retirement benefits. There is no charge for this service.

Money Coach Rule

Your goal should be to achieve the same level of income in retirement as you enjoyed in your peak earning years.

There are growing concerns about the future viability of the government's Social Security system as our population continues to age and fewer younger people contribute to it.

Contributions to the Social Security system are projected to rise substantially over the next several decades, and if future generations of voters ultimately reject higher contributions as politically unacceptable, the government may be forced to dramatically reduce the plan's payouts. As a result, Americans may have to fall back more and more on their own resources in retirement.

Some people seem to think that's okay, and they'll simply adjust their retirement lifestyle accordingly. I say you shouldn't be prepared to accept anything less in retirement than the income you enjoyed in your peak earning years!

After all, you'll have more time available (about one-quarter to one-third of your life). You've spent your whole life working and often putting off doing things you really wanted to do, like traveling. In retirement you'll have the time, but will you have the money?

Probably not, if you don't do something to supplement your income. For most people, that means achieving growth in their investments before retirement. We'll offer specific suggestions about how, starting on page 20.

Then there are those who don't have a pension at all. It's absolutely vital that these folks put money away now so they'll have a decent income when they retire and not have to rely on government checks for support.

2. To Beat Inflation and Taxes by the Widest Margin Possible

As we noted in the previous chapter, inflation and taxes are two major adversaries as we try to get ahead financially.

Your real rate of return is what you make after taxes and inflation.

It is generally agreed that a 3% *real rate of return* is pretty good; of course, the higher the better.

The problem is that many people are simply treading water.

If you put your money in a savings account or buy certificates of deposit (CDs) or U.S. savings bonds, you're probably not getting ahead financially.

Here's why:

U.S. SAVINGS BONDS

Advertised Rate of Return	5.0%
Taxes (at 40%[1])	– 2.0%
Inflation (current)	– 3.0%
Real Rate of Return	**= 0.0%**

[1] The 40% tax rate assumes a 33% marginal federal income tax rate plus 7% typical state income tax rate.

So, if seeking significant growth is your objective (as it should be), you will usually not achieve it by putting your money in the bank or by buying U.S. savings bonds or bank CDs.

Wouldn't you rather experience this?

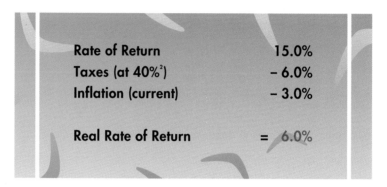

Rate of Return	15.0%
Taxes (at 40%[2])	– 6.0%
Inflation (current)	– 3.0%
Real Rate of Return	= 6.0%

Coach's Quote

"Your real rate of return is what you make after taxes and inflation."

Money Coach Rule

Start now to ensure that you're part of the minority of Americans who retire with financial dignity.

Now you're making progress. You achieved 15.0% return on investment, instead of settling for 5.0%, and your real rate of return is above that magic 3.0% level. It's an annual real gain of 6.0% rather than a zero after-tax return.

And it's easy to do. Begin building your strategy using the following steps to achieve growth.

1. START NOW!

Why start now? It's important to start now because time is a critical element in achieving growth; the earlier the better and better late than never.

Let's assume you set a goal to have $100,000 at age 65 to supplement your other sources of income at that time. Believe it or not, if you are 25 now, you can achieve this goal by saving only $8.50 per month (at 12%). Most people can find $8.50 a month if they want to, especially if they know what it will turn into at age 65.

[2] The 40% tax rate assumes a 33% marginal federal income tax rate plus 7% typical state income tax rate.

THE $100,000 QUESTION

How much you'd have to save every month to end up with $100,000 when you reach 65

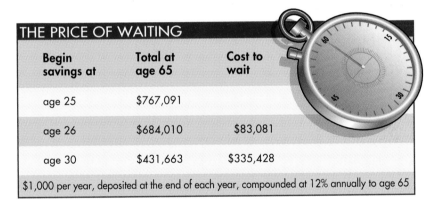

$8.50

$28.61

$101.09

$434.71

| 25 | 35 | 45 | 55 |

STARTING AGE

But if you're 55 now and want to achieve the same goal—$100,000 at age 65—you're going to have to put aside $434.71 per month (at 12%)—51 times more than you would have had to save monthly at age 25!

So it's easy to see that if you want to be financially independent, you must start now. The longer you wait, the more it will cost you to achieve your goal. Consider an annual savings program of $1,000.

Waiting five years before starting to invest $1,000 per year (from age 25 to 30) actually costs you $335,428!

THE PRICE OF WAITING

Begin savings at	Total at age 65	Cost to wait
age 25	$767,091	
age 26	$684,010	$83,081
age 30	$431,663	$335,428

$1,000 per year, deposited at the end of each year, compounded at 12% annually to age 65

2. PAY YOURSELF FIRST: USE THE 10% SOLUTION!

At the first of each month, before you pay a single bill, write yourself a check for at least 10% of your income and make it part of your regular investment program.

Who deserves it more than you do? After all, you earned it.

Why is it so vital to pay yourself first?

The discouraging truth is that many of those over 65 must now rely on welfare to see them through their retirement years. They live at subsistence levels, and the situation is substantially worse for women.

Many are also relying on Social Security benefits to assist them in their old age. First of all, these benefits will not enable most people to live at the level they did during their working career, and, second, there are fewer and fewer people contributing to Social Security in relation to the number drawing from it as time goes on and as the population ages.

It is quite possible that when you retire, Social Security will not provide a great deal toward your retirement. The United States will experience a dramatic increase in the number of seniors in the future. As a result there is no guarantee that social programs once considered universal will be continued. There is no contract with the government; programs can be drastically cut back, and there is a remote possibility that they can be wiped out.

Even if you contribute to a pension plan at work (and only about 39% of Americans do), your pension income, combined with Social Security benefits, typically will provide you with only 40% to 50% of your peak earning income. Social Security will provide only about 25% of your earnings in your peak earning years. The maximum one can currently receive is a little over $20,000 per year; most receive less. And up to 85% of what you do receive is taxed!

THE RULE OF 72

Want to know how long it will take to double your money? Just divide 72 by your investment rate of return. For example, if a mutual fund you're investing in produces an average annual compound rate of return of 12%, you will double your money in 72÷12=6 years.

RATE OF RETURN	TIME REQUIRED TO DOUBLE INVESTMENT
4%	18 years
5%	14.4 years
6%	12 years
7%	10.3 years
8%	9 years
9%	8 years
10%	7.2 years
11%	6.5 years
12%	6 years

Remember the goal: to retire at the same income level as you achieved during your peak earning years. It is unwise to rely on someone else to provide for your financial future. No one cares about your future the way you do.

3. BE CONSISTENT!

Time, as we have just seen, is one key element in achieving growth.

The other significant part of the equation is consistency—but it doesn't take much money to get started, and a little will turn into a lot.

The following chart illustrates how it works. Let's assume you can invest only $100 per month over a long term and that you can obtain a 15.0% return on your money. In 25 years it'll grow to nearly $325,000; in 35 years, to more than $1.46 million. And in 40 years, you'll have more than $3.1 million!

It sounds unbelievable, but it's true. Time and consistency are powerful! Your $100 per month (only about $23 per week) turns into $3.1 million after 40 years.

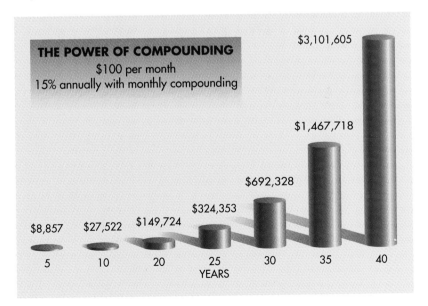

THE POWER OF COMPOUNDING
$100 per month
15% annually with monthly compounding

YEARS	Value
5	$8,857
10	$27,522
20	$149,724
25	$324,353
30	$692,328
35	$1,467,718
40	$3,101,605

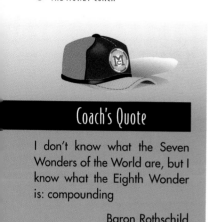

Coach's Quote

I don't know what the Seven Wonders of the World are, but I know what the Eighth Wonder is: compounding

Baron Rothschild

The growth of money over time is called "compounding." And it's one of the most amazing and exciting financial concepts of all.

Many people don't think a few extra percentage points of return amount to much money. They are wrong.

Just a few percentage points of return compounded over several years can make a difference of thousands and thousands of additional dollars. Here's how it works.

The accompanying chart shows what happens when you invest $3,500 each year for 30 years at different rates:

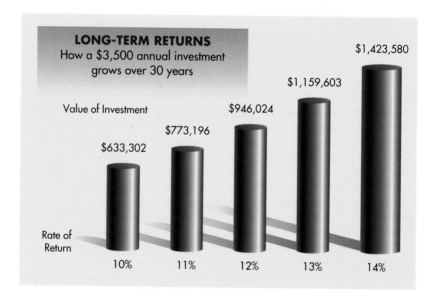

LONG-TERM RETURNS
How a $3,500 annual investment grows over 30 years

Value of Investment

$633,302 — 10%
$773,196 — 11%
$946,024 — 12%
$1,159,603 — 13%
$1,423,580 — 14%

Rate of Return

It's clear that the rate of return has a huge impact on the final amount of money available; this chart reinforces the fact that we should always seek out these few extra percentage points of return in order to achieve the greatest growth possible.

Note that a difference of only 1% (from 10% to 11%) produces an added return of about $140,000.

COACH'S PLAYBOOK

Pay off your bank loans and credit cards.

It's true that debt—a bank loan or a mort-gage—can help to focus your attention and ensure that the payments are made. It's a form of "forced savings." Many of us won't save $100 a month but will pay back a loan at $100 a month. The effect is simi-lar. However, there is a major difference. When you have a loan, you're paying inter-est on that loan! That means it's costing you money—and it's after-tax dollars.

And that is particularly true of credit cards. Several major credit cards charge in the range of 15% to 18%, and some have been higher than that. Yet, thousands of people continue to hold U.S. savings bonds or bank CDs, which are fully taxable, at the same time that they have outstanding consumer loans. No! No! No!

One more thought. If you've got more than one loan, first pay off the one that's costing you the most. If you've got a loan at 10% and one at 8%, pay off or at least reduce the 10% loan first.

Alternatively, consider consolidating two or more outstanding loans; you may be able to negotiate a lower rate than you're paying now and you may be able to reduce your monthly payments at the same time. In short, get rid of your nondeductible debt as soon as you can. It'll make you feel great, and it's one of the best moves you can make!

Money Coach Rule

Pay Yourself 10% First + Start Early + Magic of Compounding = Financial Independence

Money Coach Rule

The message should be clear: pay off car loans, furniture loans, travel loans etc., and credit card balances as soon as possible! You'll be much better positioned to ensure that you can continue to use the magic 10% solution.

4. BE AN "OWNER" – NOT A "LOANER"

I can hear you now: "Okay, Coach," you're saying, "I'll start now; I'll invest regularly, saving 10% of my salary; I'll take advantage of the magic of compounding, and I'll make the Rule of 72 work for me. But tell me, Coach, how do I get a 15% to 18% return on my money so that it doubles in four to five years?"

Achieving higher rates of return over the long term is simple. The trick is to be an owner, not a loaner.

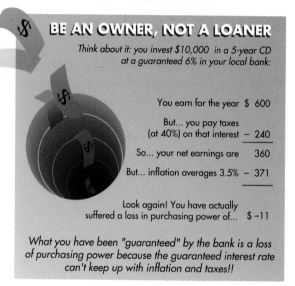

BE AN OWNER, NOT A LOANER

Think about it: you invest $10,000 in a 5-year CD at a guaranteed 6% in your local bank:

You earn for the year	$ 600
But... you pay taxes (at 40%) on that interest	– 240
So... your net earnings are	360
But... inflation averages 3.5%	– 371
Look again! You have actually suffered a loss in purchasing power of...	$ –11

What you have been "guaranteed" by the bank is a loss of purchasing power because the guaranteed interest rate can't keep up with inflation and taxes!!

What's the difference? When you're a loaner, you lend money to the government (when you buy savings bonds) or to the banks (if you put money there in term deposits or in CDs). You receive a guaranteed rate of return, have the knowledge that your money is secure, and sacrifice substantial growth potential.

But what are you really achieving? Despite the fact that many deposits in a bank or trust company are guaranteed at a fixed rate and by the Federal Deposit Insurance Corporation against loss, you may still be losing—and losing something equally important—purchasing power.

If it were consistently more advantageous for individuals and businesses to put their money in the bank than to invest in profit-seeking businesses, we would have a major problem. But that's not the case. In fact, just the opposite is true.

Despite all our complaints and the constant focus in the media on problems, we're better off than ever before. Those of us lucky enough to live in the United States, which according to a recent United Nations study is one of the best countries in the world in which to reside, are better off than 95% of the world's population.

What's more, the next several decades will bring greater opportunities for growth than ever before in the history of mankind! The way to participate in all of this is to be an owner, not a loaner.

We know now that if you're a typical loaner, you're putting your money in the bank, or purchasing CDs or government savings bonds. But what's an owner?

An owner actually invests in the growth of the economy of this country or in the growth of the economy of other countries. While many people

Money Coach Rule

To accumulate money to achieve growth, be an owner — not a loaner.

associate investment as an owner with investment in the stock market, this is not necessarily the case. It may involve ownership in mutual funds, real estate, or the stock market. The key is that traditionally, if your investment goes into ownership vehicles (stocks, mutual funds, real estate), your annual return may be 12% to 16% or even more. Take a look, for example, at the accompanying chart, which shows the growth of a $1 investment in four different asset classes made on December 31, 1925. The figures assume reinvestment of all income and do not account for taxes or transaction costs. The four assets presented here are small-company stocks, large-company stocks, long-term government bonds, and Treasury bills.

Stocks have provided the largest increase in wealth over the past 71 years by a huge margin. The $1 investment in large-company stocks increased by over 1,000 times to $1,370.95. The small-company stock investment grew to an even more impressive $4,495.99. Fixed-income investments provided only a fraction of the growth of stocks. Long-term government bonds grew to $33.73, and Treasury bills grew to only $13.54. Inflation, over the same period, caused $1 in consumer goods in 1925 to rise in price to $8.85 by the end of 1996.

From this graph it would seem that stocks were the investment of choice, as their returns far outdistanced those of bonds and cash equivalents. However, these exceptional returns came with much greater volatility than was found with any fixed-income investment. Notice the relatively steep peaks and valleys in both stock indices. This is indicative of high volatility on a month-to-month and year-to-year basis. In comparison, the bond and Treasury bill index lines are smoother and relatively free of large peaks and valleys. This illustrates the historically lower volatility of fixed-income investments.

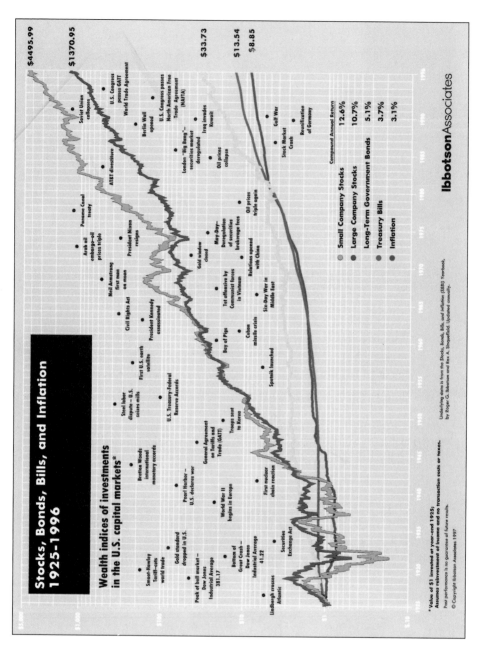

Stocks, Bonds, Bills, and Inflation
1925-1996

Wealth indices of investments
in the U.S. capital markets*

	Compound Annual Return
Small Company Stocks	12.6%
Large Company Stocks	10.7%
Long-Term Government Bonds	5.1%
Treasury Bills	3.7%
Inflation	3.1%

$4495.99
$1370.95
$33.73
$13.54
$8.85

IbbotsonAssociates

* Value of $1 invested at year-end 1925;
Assumes reinvestment of income and no transaction costs or taxes.
Past performance is no guarantee of future results.
© Copyright Ibbotson Associates 1997

Underlying data is from the Stocks, Bonds, Bills, and Inflation (SBBI) Yearbook,
by Roger G. Ibbotson and Rex A. Sinquefield. Updated annually.

It's true there are no guarantees as an owner. The element of risk is always present in any investment that holds the potential of higher gains. You could earn no income or even lose part of your original investment, especially in the short term. But many ownership vehicles available have extremely good rates of return and long successful track records. And if you want to achieve growth to maximize your return, you must accept some risk. But history is on your side. So if you want to accumulate money to achieve growth—be an owner not a loaner!

OWNERSHIP OUTPERFORMS IN THE LONG RUN

$1 Original Investment
Compounded Annually
(December 1925 to December 1996)

$1,370.95 EQUITIES

$33.73 LONG–TERM GOVT. BONDS 5.1%

$13.54 T–BILLS 3.7%

$8.85 INFLATION 3.1%

12.6%

Source: Ibbotson Associates, *Stocks, Bonds, Bills, and Inflation* 1997 Yearbook.

The chart to the left illustrates the compound annual return on investment of Treasury bills and bonds (loanership vehicles) over the past 45 years compared with the return achieved over the same period on the stock market (equities). You'll agree it's better to be an owner than a loaner.

The following chart compares asset values for 20-year holdings, 1977 through 1996, per $1 initially invested:

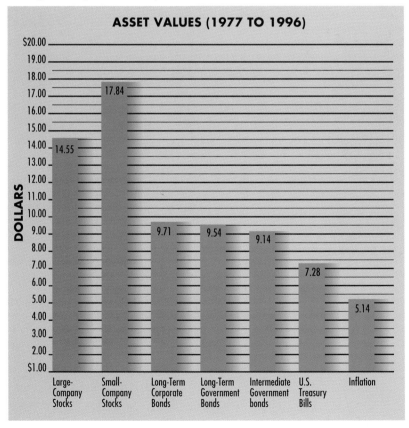

ASSET VALUES (1977 TO 1996)

Large-Company Stocks	14.55
Small-Company Stocks	17.84
Long-Term Corporate Bonds	9.71
Long-Term Government Bonds	9.54
Intermediate Government bonds	9.14
U.S. Treasury Bills	7.28
Inflation	5.14

DOLLARS

5. PUT YOUR MONEY TO WORK IN MUTUAL FUNDS

WHAT IS A MUTUAL FUND?

A mutual fund is a "pool" of money to which thousands of people contribute. This pool of money is managed by professional money managers who invest the money in a variety of financial instruments, which may include Treasury bills (T-bills), safe and secure government or corporate bonds, and shares of U.S. and foreign corporations. They keep a watchful eye on the economy, on political, demographic, and economic trends, and on international events in order to determine where and how the pool of money can be invested to produce the most solid long-term growth, within the fund's investment criteria. Funds run the gamut of the investments and risk spectrum.

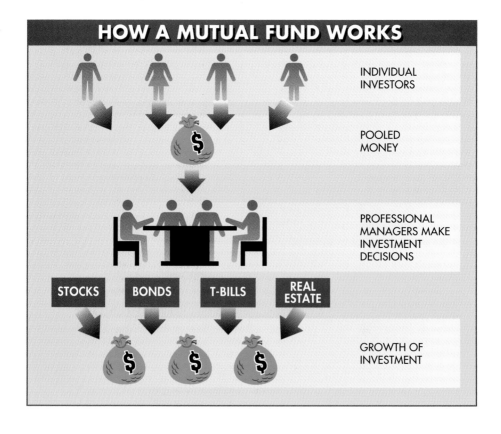

THE BENEFITS OF MUTUAL FUNDS

Professional Money Management

Most people are too busy to take time to effectively oversee their financial affairs. They are also not trained to be expert money managers. By buying mutual funds, these people are receiving the benefit of the experience and skills of some of the best money managers in the world, whose goal is to achieve long-term growth for the money they invest.

Fidelity Magellan, one of the largest and most successful funds, in reporting its investment performance since 1979, stated that $10,000 invested on December 31, 1979, would have grown to $329,964 by December 31, 1996. The annual rate of growth is more than 22.5%. This does not take into account taxes or broker fees and assumes that all distributions were reinvested in the fund, including dividends and capital gains. Fidelity Magellan was managed for many years by the legendary Peter Lynch. While this remarkable growth may be difficult to sustain in the future, the prospect is not beyond the realm of possibility. Other mutual funds have achieved growth that was only a few percentage points less over this period.

One of the most successful mutual funds ever, the Templeton Growth Fund I, which was managed by Sir John Templeton and his management team, is a good example. Those who invested $10,000 in this fund when it began in 1954 saw their investment grow to be worth over $3.2 million by 1997. That's an average annual compounded growth rate of nearly 15%!

Although the Templeton funds continue to follow his investment principles, Sir John Templeton is no longer affiliated with Franklin Templeton. He relinquished all fund-related management duties at the time of the Templeton merger in 1992 but continued to serve as chairman of the U.S.-based Templeton funds until April 16, 1995, and as the chairman of the Canadian-based Templeton Growth Fund until August 15, 1996.

You can find historical data on individual mutual funds in *Kiplinger's Mutual Funds* ($5.95 at newsstands) and *Mutual Funds* ($2.50). Another excellent source is the *Guide to Low-Load Mutual Funds* (about $20), published by the American Association of Individual Investors (AAII) in Chicago. An annual membership in AAII is well worth the $50 charge and includes the *Guide*. Excellent data on mutual funds is provided by Lipper Analytic Services (Summit, New Jersey) and by Morningstar in Chicago.

Diversification

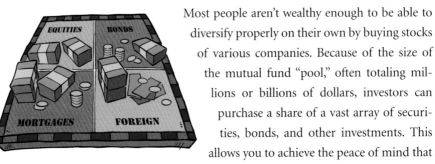

Most people aren't wealthy enough to be able to diversify properly on their own by buying stocks of various companies. Because of the size of the mutual fund "pool," often totaling millions or billions of dollars, investors can purchase a share of a vast array of securities, bonds, and other investments. This allows you to achieve the peace of mind that comes from "not putting all your eggs in one basket."

"Hands-off" Investment

As mentioned earlier, most people don't have the time, the inclination, or the expertise to do the research necessary to make wise investment decisions. This is all looked after for investors by professional money managers for whom this is a full-time job.

Lots of Choice

Regardless of your circumstances, there are mutual funds that can meet your needs. Some people want income now; others, who will require income later, opt for growth now. Some investors are aggressive, while others are much more conservative. Some select equity funds, others prefer real estate funds, and still others

like mortgage funds—or a mixture of each. Some wish to invest in specialty funds like gold; others like to invest in specific foreign regions like Japan or Europe. With several thousand funds available to select from, there is truly a fund to meet virtually every need.

In addition to these major benefits, there are other attractive features, too:

● Most funds allow initial purchases as low as $1,000 or less, with subsequent purchases as low as $1 for some funds, up to a $1,000 minimum, as shown in the accompanying chart.

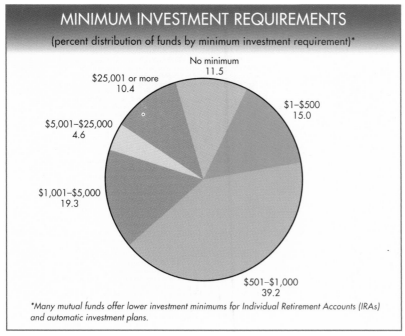

MINIMUM INVESTMENT REQUIREMENTS
(percent distribution of funds by minimum investment requirement)*

No minimum
11.5

$25,001 or more
10.4

$1–$500
15.0

$5,001–$25,000
4.6

$1,001–$5,000
19.3

$501–$1,000
39.2

*Many mutual funds offer lower investment minimums for Individual Retirement Accounts (IRAs) and automatic investment plans.

Source: Investment Company Institute (ICI), *1997 Mutual Fund Fact Book*, 37th ed. (Washington, DC: ICI, 1996), p. 29.

● Most funds make it very easy to invest with lump-sum, preauthorized checking on a regular basis or through a group purchase with automatic payroll deduction.

● Mutual funds are "liquid" and can be sold easily and quickly; there is no minimum length of time required to hold the funds.

● Many funds are structured so that there is no acquisition fee and, depending on how long you hold the fund, there may be no exit fee either.

❋ A systematic withdrawal plan that meets your individual needs can be established as you near retirement and may require regular income.

It is important to note that mutual funds should be seen as long-term investments (i.e., they should be held for at least five years). Over this extended period of time, the economy and the market will most likely continue to develop and grow, as will the value of your investments. For those willing and able to hold their shares over the long term, there will be little need for concern. But for those who might consider purchasing for a hold of only a year or two, there is a greater degree of risk, and the value of their funds might actually end up being lower than when they were purchased. For that reason, it's best to view a mutual fund as a long-term investment. When you do that, you have history on your side, for, over the long term, mutual funds (which represent ownership) have significantly outperformed CDs (which represent loanership).

What accounts for the extraordinary growth of mutual funds in the past decade? Much of it, I believe, can be attributed to an increasingly complex world that is changing so fast that few individual investors are able to function comfortably. The result has been a dramatic move in the United States and worldwide to "managed money."

For most people, this has been through mutual fund investments, although other managed-money vehicles have also emerged—including closed-end funds, REITs (real estate investment trusts), "investment" life insurance, limited partnerships, and private money management.

The trend toward managed money—although certainly helped by low interest rates and generally positive market conditions—has been driven largely by the growing number of people who recognize that they are no longer restricted to the traditional choice of CDs, U.S. savings bonds, Treasury bills, or term deposits on one hand and direct stock market investment on the other. It's based as well on an understanding that an extra single-percentage-point return, when compounded over the long term, can yield significantly more accumulated wealth; and it's based on a belief that a full-time professional will almost always achieve better investment results than a part-time amateur.

All of these events have contributed to phenomenal growth in the mutual fund industry.

According to the Investment Company Institute, mutual funds since the early 1980s have undergone a much-publicized period of growth, with almost uninterrupted increases in sales and assets. But, in the midst of the remarkable success, perhaps just as notable has been the industry's cultivation of investors interested in long-term funds.

Several decades ago, a mutual fund investment was assumed to be an investment in stocks. As the 1980s began, however, fund assets were more heavily concentrated in money market funds, the result of rising interest rates, low stock prices, and economic recession. Introduced in 1972, money market funds had become highly popular by providing investors with market-rate yields as interest rates surged to double digits in the late 1970s. The current mutual fund asset distribution is shown by the chart below.

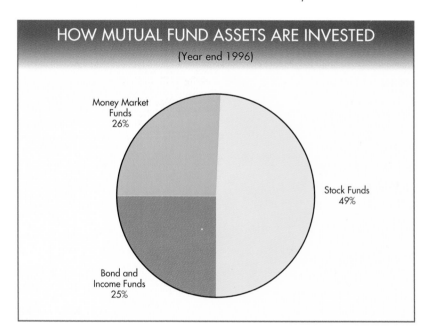

HOW MUTUAL FUND ASSETS ARE INVESTED
(Year end 1996)

Money Market Funds 26%

Stock Funds 49%

Bond and Income Funds 25%

Source: Investment Company Institute (ICI), *1997 Mutual Fund Fact Book,* 37th ed., p. 22.

By the end of 1996, investor preference had changed dramatically, with nearly three-quarters of mutual fund assets invested in long-term—especially equity—funds. Equity funds accounted for 50% of industry assets as 1997 began, double the figure recorded ten years earlier. Over the same period, fixed-income funds' share dropped significantly.

Mutual funds of all varieties have prospered in the 1980s and 1990s. For example, total industry assets skyrocketed from $716.3 billion at the end of 1986 to a record $3.54 trillion by the end of 1996, as shown in the chart below.

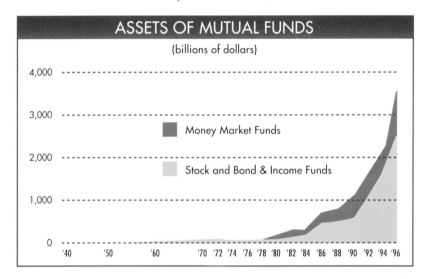

ASSETS OF MUTUAL FUNDS
(billions of dollars)

Source: Investment Company Institute (ICI), *1997 Mutual Fund Fact Book,* 37th ed., p. 16.

Equity fund asset growth increased the most, from $161.5 billion in 1986 to an all-time high of more than $1.7 trillion by the end of 1996. Bond and income fund assets rose more than half a trillion dollars for the same time period, from $262.6 billion to a record-high $886 billion. Taxable money market fund assets have more than tripled since 1986—from $228.3 billion to a record $761 billion at the end of 1996—and tax-exempt money fund assets more than doubled, to an all-time high of $140.1 billion. These figures are shown in the following table.

			Taxable	Tax-Exempt	
		Bond and	Money	Money	
Year	Equity Funds	Income Funds	Market Funds	Market Funds	Total

Total Mutual Fund Industry Net Assets (billions of dollars)

Year	Equity Funds	Bond and Income Funds	Taxable Money Market Funds	Tax-Exempt Money Market Funds	Total
1970	$45.1	$2.5	—	—	$47.6
1971	51.6	3.4	—	—	55.0
1972	55.9	3.9	—	—	59.8
1973	43.0	3.5	—	—	46.5
1974	30.9	3.2	$1.7	—	35.8
1975	37.5	4.7	3.7	—	45.9
1976	39.2	8.4	3.7	—	51.3
1977	34.0	11.0	3.9	—	48.9
1978	32.7	12.3	10.9	—	55.9
1979	35.9	13.1	45.2	$0.3	94.5
1980	44.4	14.0	74.5	1.9	134.8
1981	41.2	14.0	181.9	4.3	241.4
1982	53.7	23.2	206.6	13.2	296.7
1983	77.0	36.6	162.5	16.8	292.9
1984	83.1	54.0	209.7	23.8	370.6
1985	116.9	134.8	207.5	36.3	495.5
1986	161.5	262.6	228.3	63.8	716.2
1987	180.7	273.1	254.7	61.4	769.9
1988	194.8	277.5	272.3	65.7	810.3
1989	249.1	304.8	358.7	69.4	982.0
1990	245.8	322.7	414.7	83.6	1,066.8
1991	411.6	441.4	452.6	89.9	1,395.5
1992	522.8	577.3	451.4	94.8	1,646.3
1993	749.0	761.1	461.9	103.4	2,075.4
1994	866.5	684.0	500.4	110.6	2,161.5
1995	1,269.0	798.3	629.7	123.3	2,820.3
1996	1,750.9	886.5	761.7	140.1	3,539.2

Source: Investment Company Institute (ICI), *1997 Mutual Fund Fact Book,* 37th ed., p. 60.

• TYPES OF MUTUAL FUNDS •

1. Equity Funds (also referred to as Common Stock Funds or Growth Funds)

Equity Funds invest primarily in common shares of corporations. The equity funds available range from the very conservative blue chip funds to speculative or venture funds. Equity funds vary in the level of diversification and risk involved, but most funds have growth as their major investment objective. Historically, returns on common shares have outperformed fixed-income securities. However, on a year-to-year basis, common share returns can be volatile. Some equity funds also generate dividend income. When the personality of the fund is to do both—earn dividends and grow—it will be described as a **growth and income** fund.

2. Bond and Income Funds

Bond funds primarily invest in government and corporate bonds and debentures, but many hold other fixed-income securities. The objective is to provide income as well as the safety afforded by government and corporate debt securities. Bond funds have moderate growth potential, especially when interest rates decline.

Income or mortgage funds invest primarily in mortgages, as well as in other fixed-income securities, such as bonds, and mortgage-backed securities. The objective is to provide attractive income returns versus other fixed-income securities (i.e., term deposits, CDs, etc.), with a high degree of safety.

3. Money Market Funds: Taxable or Tax-Exempt

Money market funds invest in short-term money market instruments, such as Treasury bills, whose maturities are less than one year. The objective is to provide a better return than savings accounts with minimal risk of capital. Money market instruments are very safe and have the highest available credit ratings among securities. These funds offer safety and liquidity.

There are many other variations of funds. Each type, classified by investment objective, is shown in the following table.

TYPES OF MUTUAL FUNDS

Stock Funds

Aggressive Growth Funds seek maximum capital growth; current income is not a significant factor. These funds invest in stocks out of the mainstream, such as new companies, companies fallen on hard times, or industries temporarily out of favor. They may use investment techniques involving greater than average risk.

Growth Funds seek capital growth; dividend income is not a significant factor. They invest in the common stock of well-established companies.

Growth and Income Funds seek to combine long-term capital growth and current income. These funds invest in the common stock of companies whose share value has increased and that have displayed a solid record of paying dividends.

Precious Metals/Gold Funds seek capital growth. Their portfolios are invested primarily in securities associated with gold and other precious metals.

International Funds seek growth in the value of their investments. Their portfolios are invested primarily in stocks of companies located outside the U.S.

Global Equity Funds seek growth in the value of their investments. They invest in stocks traded worldwide, including those in the U.S.

Income-Equity Funds seek a high level of income by investing primarily in stocks of companies with good dividend-paying records.

Bond and Income Funds

Flexible Portfolio Funds allow their money managers to anticipate or respond to changing market conditions by investing in stocks or bonds or money market instruments, depending on economic changes.

Balanced Funds generally seek to conserve investors' principal, pay current income, and achieve long-term growth of principal and income. Their portfolios are a mix of bonds, preferred stocks, and common stocks.

Income-Mixed Funds seek a high level of income. These funds invest in income-producing securities, including stocks and bonds.

Income-Bond Funds seek a high level of current income. These funds invest in a mix of corporate and government bonds.

U.S. Government Income Funds seek current income. They invest in a variety of government securities, including U.S. Treasury bonds, federally guaranteed mortgage-backed securities, and other government notes.

GNMA (Ginnie Mae) Funds seek a high level of income. The majority of their portfolios is invested in mortgage securities backed by the Government National Mortgage Association (GNMA).

Global Bonds Funds seek a high level of income. These funds invest in debt securities of companies and countries worldwide, including those in the U.S.

Corporate Bond Funds seek a high level of income. The majority of their portfolios is invested in corporate bonds, with the balance in U.S. Treasury bonds or bonds issued by a federal agency.

High-yield Bond Funds seek a very high yield, but carry a greater degree of risk than corporate bond funds. The majority of their portfolios is invested in lower-rated corporate bonds.

National Municipal Bond Funds—Long-term seek income that is not taxed by the federal government. They invest in bonds issued by states and municipalities to finance schools, highways, hospitals, bridges, and other municipal works.

State Municipal Bond Funds—Long-term seek income that is exempt from both federal and state tax for residents of that state. They invest in bonds issued by a single state.

Money Market Funds

Taxable Money Market Funds seek to maintain a stable net asset value. These funds invest in the short-term, high-grade securities sold in the money market, such as U.S. Treasury bills, certificates of deposit of large banks, and commercial paper. The average maturity of their portfolios is limited to 90 days or less.

Tax-exempt Money Market Funds—National seek income that is not taxed by the federal government with minimum risk. They invest in municipal securities with relatively short maturities.

Tax-exempt Money Market Funds—State seek income that is exempt from federal tax and state tax for residents of that state. They invest in municipal securities with relatively short maturities issued by a single state.

Source: Investment Company Institute (ICI), *1997 Mutual Fund Fact Book*, 37th ed., pp.24-25.

THE BEST WAYS TO INVEST IN MUTUAL FUNDS

Depending on your investment style, your level of expertise, and the amount of time you feel you can afford to devote to managing your portfolio personally, several investment strategies may be of interest and of help.

THE "DOLLAR COST AVERAGING" STRATEGY

This is probably the best and simplest way for people to invest in mutual funds.

Ideally, every investor seeks to buy at a low price and sell at a higher price at a later date. The question is how to do that, given the fact that there are market fluctuations. Nobody seems to mind the upward trends; it's those slides that upset us so much. However, by using a simple strategy called "dollar cost averaging," even the downside fluctuations can actually work to your advantage! It's as close as one can get to infallible investing—and most people don't even know about it.

Psychologically, if you are committed to regular investments and if you are prepared to invest over the long term, then downward trends (which are bound to come along) are simply opportunities to buy additional shares at lower-than-usual prices. As always, of course, the upward trends will continue to be rewarding and satisfying.

Let's see how it actually works by using the following three examples. We're going to invest $100 a month for nine years (i.e., $10,800 will be invested).

SCENARIO ONE

Because the unit prices constantly increase, the number of units purchased each year actually declines, as the chart shows. For example, in year one, the unit price is $6.00, and therefore $1,200 per year ($100 per month) buys 200 units. By the end of year six, the

unit price has increased to $8.50, and therefore $1,200 buys only 141 units. At the end of nine years, when the unit price is $10, the value of the portfolio is $13,869—a 28% increase.

SCENARIO TWO

Notice here that for the first five years, the unit price declines. Imagine how happy you'd be in that situation! But patience is rewarded. The result of lower unit prices is that a larger number of units are purchased while you continue to invest $100 per month. Note that in Scenario Two the original pur-

chase price and the final purchase price are the same ($6). There is no market rise at all.

Money Coach Rule

Use dollar cost averaging as an effective system for buying mutual funds (or stocks) on a regular basis (usually monthly) with a fixed amount of money (usually $100 – $300).

Despite this, 2,150 units have been acquired in this scenario. And even at a $6 unit price at the end of nine years, the value of the portfolio is $12,898—a 19% increase. Significant growth in the value of your investment actually occurs in a declining and recovering market. You get the benefit of purchasing more mutual fund units when prices are at a reduced value.

SCENARIO THREE

Here the unit price increases and decreases over time. Therefore, more units are purchased with the $1,200 in some years than in others. This example is probably the most realistic in reflecting actual conditions. After nine years, the number of units purchased is greater than in Scenario One—1,479 to be exact. At $10 per unit at the end of year nine, the investment is worth $14,787—a 37% increase in value.

Thus you can see that the psychological barrier of purchasing more shares when prices are low (and that's the very best time to buy) is overcome by using dollar cost averaging. In fact, dollar cost averaging removes the problem of timing from investment management. By investing regularly, we don't get hung up on timing, for we've now got a logical comprehensive investment strategy based on confidence in the long-term health of the U.S. and international economies.

For most people, dollar cost averaging is the best way to invest.

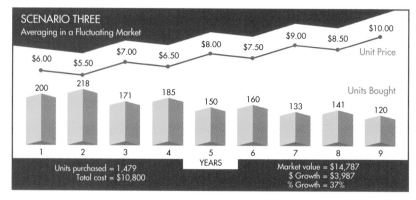

• COACH'S PLAYBOOK •

The "Best" Time to Invest

How can you predict the "BEST" vs. the "WORST" time to invest? In some cases it just may not matter!

The illustrations below cover 24 years and the "BEST/WORST" days on which to have invested twenty-four different $5,000 net investments totaling $125,000. The results in each case can be helpful in deciding when to invest.

These are the results of having invested $5,000 in Templeton Growth Fund I for each of 24 years on the day the Dow Jones Industrial Average reached its highest point of the year—the peak for stock prices each year.

Date of Market High	Cumulative Investment	Value of Account on December 31
12/29/70	$5,000	$4,511
4/28/71	10,000	10,944
12/11/72	15,000	25,729
1/11/73	20,000	27,442
3/13/74	25,000	28,246
7/15/75	30,000	43,509
9/21/76	35,000	70,051
1/03/77	40,000	90,057
9/08/78	45,000	111,698
10/05/79	50,000	146,372
11/20/80	55,000	188,937
4/27/81	60,000	192,964
12/27/82	65,000	218,670
11/29/83	70,000	295,493
1/06/84	75,000	306,781
12/16/85	80,000	396,943
12/02/86	85,000	486,140
8/25/87	90,000	505,026
10/21/88	95,000	629,031
10/09/89	100,000	775,794
7/16/90	105,000	709,687
12/31/91	110,000	936,929
6/01/92	115,000	981,248
12/29/93	120,000	1,307,090
01/31/94	125,000	1,322,557
	Value of acct. on 12/31/95	1,584,847
	Value of acct. on 12/31/96	1,910,566
Average annual rate of return: 16.11%		

Source: Franklin Templeton Group

These are the results of having invested $5,000 in Templeton Growth Fund I for each of the 24 years on the day the Dow Jones Industrial Average reached its lowest point of the year—the <u>bottom for stock prices</u> each year.

Date of Market Low	Cumulative Investment	Value of Account on December 31
5/26/70	$5,000	$4,846
11/23/71	10,000	11,513
1/26/72	15,000	27,368
12/03/73	20,000	29,685
12/06/74	25,000	30,910
1/02/75	30,000	49,022
1/02/76	35,000	78,890
11/02/77	40,000	101,958
2/28/78	45,000	127,361
11/07/79	50,000	166,922
4/21/80	55,000	216,754
9/25/81	60,000	221,488
8/12/82	65,000	252,013
1/03/83	70,000	341,466
7/24/84	75,000	354,379
1/04/85	80,000	459,174
1/22/86	85,000	562,610
10/19/87	90,000	584,586
1/20/88	95,000	728,515
1/03/89	100,000	898,894
10/11/90	105,000	822,645
1/09/91	110,000	1,087,001
10/09/92	115,000	1,138,096
01/20/93	120,000	1,516,751
04/04/94	125,000	1,534,319
Value of acct. on 12/31/95		1,838,605
Value of acct. on 12/31/96		2,216,477

Average annual rate of return: 16.86%

Source: Franklin Templeton Group

Most investors would find the results in each case quite acceptable. As a result, it appears that the "Best" Time to Invest is Whenever You Have The Money!

These illustrations represent the results of net investments. The rate of return and market value of an investment in the Fund will fluctuate, so that shares redeemed may be worth more or less than their original cost. The market is represented by the Dow Jones Industrial Average of 30 Stocks.

THE "BUY-AND-HOLD" STRATEGY

This approach is similar to dollar cost averaging except that in this strategy, the investment may not be made as regularly.

Assuming you've done your research or had the benefit of the advice of a financial advisor, there's a strong argument for picking a fund, investing the money and getting on with your life.

Templeton Growth Fund I is a classic example of a buy-and-hold fund. A $10,000 investment in this fund in November 1954—with no subsequent contributions or withdrawals—was worth over $3.2 million in 1997. You could have been Rip Van Winkle and slept for over 40 years and done very well with Templeton Growth Fund I.

But even if your interest is to "buy and hold," you probably aren't comfortable ignoring the investment completely. So to monitor it, we suggest you look for changes in the fund's management or for changes to its investment philosophy and, of course, continue to be aware of its performance compared to others in its category.

The buy-and-hold strategy isn't as exciting as some others, but if you can find a true "buy-and-hold" fund you'll be a happy investor.

THE "BOB-AND-WEAVE" STRATEGY

This approach is quite the opposite of buy-and-hold and dollar cost averaging. It's based on a belief that we as individuals can anticipate certain trends, developments, or events, and can "bob and weave" or switch among funds and asset categories to take advantage of them.

Most fund companies now allow you to switch from one of their funds to another—generally at no cost, although a fund's prospectus often provides for a fee of up to 2%. Some of the no-load funds charge an administration fee each time you do so after a certain number of "free" switches.

Now it's true that certain asset categories tend to do better at different times in the economic cycle. For example, when interest rates are falling, government bonds will tend to do well; when interest rates are low, equities will likely do well; and, when rates are rising, a cash-type investment may perform best.

But we believe very strongly that you should hold a balanced portfolio. So we urge that the "bob-and-weave" approach not be taken too far. Sure, there could be strategic times to rebalance; but those who attempt to be "market timers" do not consistently come out on top. It's a risky strategy and one that we urge be used with caution—probably as part of ongoing discussions with your financial advisor.

THE ASSET ALLOCATION STRATEGY

The asset allocation approach is a much more disciplined and more effective strategy than the bob-and-weave. In this strategy, the overall mix between fixed-income assets and equities is determined by your age and aggressiveness as an investor. (For more about asset allocation, see pages 53–56.) Then the specific components of the portfolio are selected and "plugged in" to the overall framework.

Remember, the research shows very clearly that the overall mix between equities and fixed income is the single most important investment decision we make. All other variables, including market timing, are of very little importance.

Of course, it will be necessary to rebalance your portfolio from time to time, particularly if one asset category has done extremely well in the past year. If it has, it may have grown to a larger-than-appropriate percentage of the portfolio.

Another reason to adjust your portfolio may be advancing age. We believe that, as you age (and all other things being equal), the relative weighting of fixed-income assets in your portfolio should grow. Some investors become more (or less) aggressive over the years—for a whole variety of reasons—and this change must be reflected in the overall holdings.

Finally, as indicated above, certain economic conditions lend themselves to shifts in the weighting of certain asset categories that may not otherwise be appropriate.

The main point here is that changes made to a balanced portfolio should be the result of a well-considered set of plans and have little to do with an attempt to time the market—which is more a part of the bob-and-weave approach.

THE LEVERAGING STRATEGY

This is an aggressive strategy with great upside potential—as well as some significant risk. The theory is to use other people's money—usually a bank or broker loan—adding it to yours and investing the entire amount. What you owe is increased by interest charges, or may be reduced by monthly payments, while the overall investment grows in value.

Let's assume you take $20,000 of your own money and borrow another $80,000 to make a $100,000 investment. Let's assume your investment grows by 20% to $120,000. You still owe $80,000 (plus interest), so you "own" $40,000 of the investment. Although the value of the portfolio grew by only 20%, your "stake" actually doubled from $20,000 to $40,000—a 100% increase! (Minus the interest on your loan.)

It can get even better. Assuming you borrowed the money to invest outside your tax-sheltered retirement program, the interest you pay the bank to finance the loan may be tax deductible. And assuming that you selected investments that generate tax-advantaged dividends or capital gains, your after-tax returns will be better still. Capital gains are still taxed at a maximum of 28%, which is less than the top rate on ordinary income.

So far, we've seen only the rosy side of leveraging. But there's another side that must be considered. Let's assume our $100,000 declines in value by 20% to $80,000. That represents the entire amount of your contribution to the total investment. So your original $20,000 will have been wiped out—for a pretty frightening loss of 100%! And you will owe interest on the $80,000.

Given the potential dangers inherent in leveraging strategies, we suggest that you adhere to the following guidelines:

● Borrow to a maximum of 50% of the total investment.

● Be sure cash flow will allow ongoing loan payments; don't expect to pay the loan back from profits.

● Try to avoid securing the loan with other assets, especially your home; unsecured loans are widely available at slightly higher rates (but the interest is fully deductible).

THE TAX-EFFICIENT STRATEGY

Tax-Efficient/Inefficient Portfolio

Suppose you wish to allocate your assets equally between growth stocks and corporate bonds. Further, you have half your assets in a tax-sheltered retirement program (TSRP), and the other half is outside the retirement program.

To have a tax-efficient portfolio, place your bonds in the tax-sheltered program. Though the bonds pay taxable interest, it is tax-deferred within the retirement account until you withdraw your money, and then you will be retired and probably in a lower tax bracket.

Growth stocks should be outside the TSRP. Because they pay little or no dividends, there is no current income tax. As for the capital gain, you can control the timing of sales. The gain can be realized in a year of your choice when it causes you the least taxation. Under current tax law the capital gain is forgiven upon death, so these assets can be passed on to your heirs without capital gains taxation.

The charts below show the difference between a tax-inefficient portfolio, which has the investment vehicles reversed, and a tax-efficient portfolio. It assumes, for illustration purposes, that both growth stocks and bonds offer a 10% return, the stocks through growth and the bonds through taxable interest. The tax-efficient portfolio earns 10% after tax, whereas the inefficient portfolio earns only 8%. The difference can be highly significant, especially with compounding over a long period of time.

TAX-INEFFICIENT PORTFOLIO			
ASSET CLASS	TSRP	NON-TSRP	TOTAL
Growth stocks ($100,000 @ 10%)	$10,000	0	$10,000
Bonds ($100,000 @ 10%)	0	$10,000	$10,000
Income tax at 40%	0	– $4,000	– $4,000
Total after tax	$10,000	$6,000	$16,000
After-tax return: $16,000/$200,000 = 8%			

TAX-EFFICIENT PORTFOLIO			
ASSET CLASS	TSRP	NON-TSRP	TOTAL
Growth stocks ($100,000 @ 10%)	0	$10,000	$10,000
Bonds ($100,000 @ 10%)	$10,000	0	$10,000
Income tax at 40%	0	0	0
Total after tax	$10,000	$10,000	$20,000
After-tax return: $20,000/$200,000 = 10%			

The message is that, where possible, you should hold assets that are fully taxed (fixed-income) inside the TSRP and more favorably taxed assets (growth stocks) outside the TSRP.

While this illustrates the effect of a tax-efficient portfolio, a paramount concern is wealth building. The illustration assumes that stocks and bonds both pay 10%, which is not realistic; historically, the low dividend rate of stocks is greatly enhanced by their potential for capital gains. So over the long haul, an asset allocation weighted toward stocks may prove more lucrative than bonds. The tax-efficient illustration does demonstrate that if you are to have a mixture of stocks and bonds, with investments in both tax-sheltered and non-sheltered plans, put the bonds in the tax-sheltered account because bonds generate more current taxable income than stocks.

WHAT KIND OF FUND IS RIGHT FOR YOU?

LET'S START WITH YOUR AGE

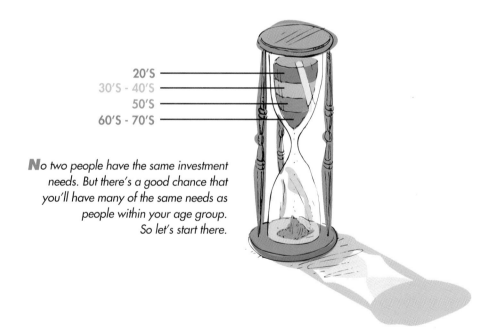

20'S
30'S - 40'S
50'S
60'S - 70'S

No two people have the same investment needs. But there's a good chance that you'll have many of the same needs as people within your age group. So let's start there.

Perhaps you're just completing your education, establishing a home of your own, or starting a family. Either way, you'll have plenty of bills. And you'll need a savings plan to meet these obligations. But if you do have any excess cash, think about putting it into a TSRP or other investment that offers long-term growth potential.

With fewer debts and more assets, you're starting to make some progress. This is the time to be looking at growth-oriented "ownership" investments. Why? Because historically they have offered superior growth rates over the long term.

Your work earnings are probably at (or near) their peak. And with the mortgage paid off (as it should be by now), you have more of that income available for investment. Growth is still important, but, with retirement in sight, you'll need to start thinking of balancing your fund portfolio with income-producing investments.

Now you're ready to enjoy the rewards of a lifetime's work. Your investment needs will shift more to security and income. But you will still require some growth investments to provide a necessary hedge against inflation.

WEIGH YOUR NEEDS FOR SECURITY, INCOME, AND GROWTH

Considerations based on age, your personal need for security, income, and growth—as well as your tolerance for risk—will also influence your choice of mutual funds. After all, it's not worth investing in a top-performing growth fund if you're going to lie awake at night worrying that it might decline in value.

Basically, it all comes down to understanding yourself, and picking the type of fund that meets your personal needs. To assist in this process, consider the following statements. If you agree with a statement, mark an "x" on the left side of the scale. If you don't agree, mark it on the right. If you're not sure, mark both sides.

AGREE DISAGREE

○ ○ ● Growth is my key investment objective right now. Income is less important.

○ ○ ● I'm interested in getting some tax relief from my investments.

○ ○ ● I understand that growth opportunities sometimes involve short-term risk.

○ ○ ● Investing is a long-term proposition for me. What I buy today, I don't expect to sell tomorrow.

○ ○ ● I recognize that, historically, "ownership" investments have provided better long-term rates of return than "loanership" investments. I want to be an "owner."

If you agree with all or most of the above statements you tend to be aggressive in your investment outlook. Conversely if you disagree your tendencies are probably conservative.

BALANCING YOUR MUTUAL FUND OBJECTIVES

Conservative.

Although you'll probably want to maintain a core portfolio of term deposits and CDs, you may want to investigate the potentially higher returns offered by income-oriented investments such as money market funds or bond and income funds.

Moderate.

Security and income are important to you, but not to the point of excluding the higher potential returns offered by some growth investments. In this case, you should consider balanced funds, asset allocation funds, or your own combination of income and growth funds.

Aggressive.

You want growth, and you have the time available to achieve it. A little short-term risk doesn't bother you if it means higher potential returns over the long term. You also want more dividends and capital gains in order to improve your after-tax return on non-TSRP investments. To meet these requirements, consider growth or equity funds and dividend funds.

FUNDS DO BETTER

NEW INDEX TELLS BY HOW MUCH

Tempted to abandon mutual funds for the seemingly greener pastures of CDs? Think again. Over the past 15 years, or about four full market cycles, mutual funds have outperformed CDs.

By how much is revealed by Lipper Analytical Services, Inc., a mutual fund tracking service in Summit, New Jersey. From March 31, 1982, through March 31, 1997, the Lipper Indices reveal the following growth rates.

Lipper Fund Index	Annual Total Return
Lipper High Yield Bond Fund	12.3%
Lipper Growth Fund Index	15.34%
Lipper Growth and Income Fund Index	15.93%

In dollars, a $1,000 investment would have grown to $5,698, $8,505, or $9,182, respectively, for the three types of funds in 15 years. By contrast, a 6% bank CD would have grown to only $2,397.

From the indexes' 15-year history, investors can glean three important lessons. The first is that mutual funds "collectively" deliver excellent value. They not only do better than CDs, they have often outperformed the Dow Jones Industrial Average including dividends, and they have clobbered inflation. Not just over some lucky period when things were going well, but over a long time, through periods of inflation, deflation, war, recessions, high interest rates, and boom times.

The second lesson is that a balanced portfolio is the best blend of risk and return. The Growth and Income Fund Index is representative of such a portfolio because it is made up of all investments. (The index excludes money market funds, because they're just another way of holding cash.)

A balanced portfolio manages to capture much of the extra return offered by equities without much of the risk. Magic? No, it's just plain math. Because some asset classes zig while others zag, balanced investors enjoy a smoother ride.

The third lesson from the 15-year history of the Lipper Indices: Don't even try to time the market. Even during the recession of 1990–1991, contrary to what you might expect with the benefit of hindsight, the Indices did well.

Instead of moving in and out of the market, hang in and put the market to work for you.

These types of results aren't an exaggeration of the merit of mutual funds. If anything, the Lipper Indices are an accurate growth yardstick. Because they include many funds, they are a reasonable indicator of how much you should be able to make without taking big risks, picking strong-performing funds, or adding value in any other way.

The truth is, bad funds do exist. But many have been folded or merged with another fund. When that happens, the poor record vanishes and the merged fund adopts the record of the better fund. The Lipper Indices include those poor funds, thus avoiding the upward bias of the monthly fund averages.

An index composed of many funds also avoids other selection biases. It doesn't just pick the good performers, or restrict itself to the big funds, which tend to do a little better than the overall fund universe.

In short, the Lipper Indices provide a snapshot of the big picture, something that investors often lose sight of. Especially during difficult times like we experienced in 1990 and the early part of 1991.

But the truth is, funds do better!

THE IMPORTANCE OF ASSET ALLOCATION

What is the most critical factor in successful mutual fund investing? Like many people, you may believe that it all depends on picking the "right" fund—the one with the best numbers. But as most fund managers know, consistently high returns do not depend on putting money into specific securities; rather, it depends on putting money into the right types of securities. The same rule applies to mutual fund investing: Put your money into the right fund categories, and chances are you'll be farther ahead in the long run.

The categories of funds you choose—and the weighting of each category relative to the portfolio as a whole—is known as **asset allocation**. And Nobel Prize–winning research has shown that it accounts for between 85% and 92% of total portfolio returns. (By contrast, the same research puts the contribution of security selection—that is, choice of specific investments—at only about 2%!)

Clearly, the overriding decision in the development of any investment portfolio is the mix of assets within it. Traditionally, however, individual investors have given the **least** consideration to this **most important** decision.

Conversely, the selection of individual components (securities) is of relatively little importance. Yet investors usually spend the most time and energy in making this **least significant** decision.

WHAT ASSET CATEGORIES SHOULD BE INCLUDED?

A well balanced portfolio should include the following:

Fixed-income investments, such as:

● **Cash or cash equivalents** (checking accounts, passbook savings accounts, Treasury bills) to provide liquidity for an emergency or an opportunity

● **U.S. Treasury bonds** for stability and high income

● **International bonds** for protection against U.S. currency risk

Equity (stock) investments, such as:

● **U.S. equities**, to participate in U.S. growth via a number of world-class success stories

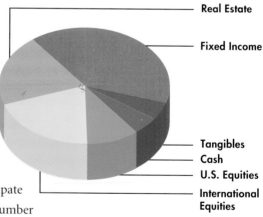

Real Estate

Fixed Income

Tangibles

Cash

U.S. Equities

International Equities

- **International equities**, to hedge the "dollar risk" and to enjoy the broadest possible range of investment choices

- **Real estate**, for inflation protection with tax benefits and income

- **Precious metals**, including gold, for protection from inflation and crisis

- **Oil and gas**, for inflation protection with tax benefits and income

WHAT'S THE RIGHT BALANCE FOR ME?

There is no "perfect" asset mix that's right for every investor. It will vary from person to person, depending on factors such as time horizon, investment objectives, and risk tolerance.

Here are some guidelines that will help you identify the mix that's right for you:

1. Start with your age:

   The total percentage of your portfolio held in fixed-income investments (i.e., cash and cash equivalents, as well as government and corporate bonds) should approximately match your age. So if you have a $100,000 portfolio and you are 40 years old, about $40,000 should be in fixed income.

2. Assess your risk tolerance:

   Imagine a scale ranging from 1 to 10, where a "1" represents the most pathologically cautious, nervous type of investor—the sort of person who keeps their money under the mattress because they're certain the banks will collapse. A "10" is (or would like to be) a professional gambler.

   Which number are you? Our experience is that everyone has an intuitive sense of where they fall on the scale.

3. Adjust your fixed-income percentage:

   Here we combine the previous two factors: age and risk tolerance.

   If your risk tolerance is in the middle of the scale at "5," then make no adjustment to the fixed-income component of your portfolio based on your age.

   For every number **higher** than 5, reduce the fixed-income component by 5%. For example, if you are 40 years old and rate yourself a "7" on the risk tolerance scale, reduce your fixed-income component by 10%—in this case, from 40% to 30%.

For every number **lower** than 5, add 5% to the fixed-income component. For example, if you are 40 years old and rate yourself a "2" on the risk tolerance scale, increase your fixed-income component by 15%—in this case, from 40% to 55%.

Notice that the effect of these guidelines is to increase the conservative component of our portfolio as we age and become less aggressive.

HOW DO WE KNOW THAT THIS BALANCE WILL WORK?

Well, history is on our side, as you'll see. A portfolio has been developed for an investor with 53% stocks, 7% bonds, and 40% Treasury bills in her portfolio. A balanced portfolio offers a number of major advantages.

The bottom line for the balanced portfolio is that it can provide **above-average returns** with **reduced** risk, and offer **preferred tax treatment** at the same time. My experience is that investors who can obtain all three of these advantages are very happy indeed.

Clearly, there's a lot to be said for developing the right balance among asset categories.

For many people, a properly balanced portfolio represents the means by which they can participate in the growth and favorable tax treatment of several asset types. At the same time, they enjoy the peace of mind that comes from having an investment that (in our example) has not declined in value during any one of the past 20 years.

THE IMPORTANCE OF DIVERSIFICATION

A Nobel Prize was awarded recently for research related to investments. The prize-winning conclusion: It's better not to "put all your eggs in one basket!" Sounds simple, and it is. But what does it mean for individuals and why is it so important?

I've already discussed the concept of a balanced portfolio—where that balance is achieved by weighting your holdings across various asset categories. There are other ways to diversify, too, some of which I've discussed earlier in the book.

As our portfolio becomes appropriately balanced, it becomes more diversified, and there are major advantages to this diversification.

The accompanying chart shows how diversifying across asset categories helps to reduce risk. Notice that with one asset category in a portfolio (that is, "all your eggs in one basket"), the risk (measured by standard deviation) is about 15%. With each additional asset category, the risk declines so that with representation in eight asset categories (and there really aren't many more) it's cut almost in half, to 9%.

Similarly, when dealing with stocks only, unsystematic risk is substantially reduced by going from owning one stock to owning 128 (although research shows that after 50 stocks are in a portfolio, subsequent additions reduce risk only minimally).

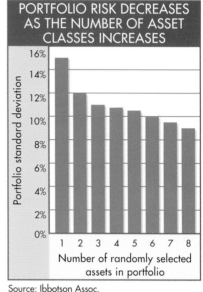

PORTFOLIO RISK DECREASES AS THE NUMBER OF ASSET CLASSES INCREASES

Portfolio standard deviation (vertical axis: 0% to 16%)

Number of randomly selected assets in portfolio (horizontal axis: 1 to 8)

Source: Ibbotson Assoc.

Essentially, diversification is a conservative strategy that acknowledges that we will not always be right in our selection of securities, geographic location, or manager; by not overweighting our position in any one of these, the negative impact of being wrong is reduced. Once we acknowledge that we will not be right all the time, we are able to adjust our thinking to achieve more consistent (if less spectacular) growth and avoid big (and potentially devastating) losses.

CONSIDER INTERNATIONAL DIVERSIFICATION

Effective diversification is achieved by holding different asset classes, often including geographical diversity. The trend to international investing is growing rapidly and with good reason.

Fortunately for Americans, financial opportunities in U.S. investments abound. There are more than 2,000 securities listed on the New York Stock Exchange, and thousands more trade on the American Exchange and NASDAQ. There are nearly 10,000 mutual funds to choose from. Our choices are plentiful. Stocks from many foreign countries are traded in the United States, so we can easily buy stock in European, Australian, Asian, South and Central American, Canadian, and Mexican companies.

Still, let's remember that the United States represents less than 30% of the world's markets. In other words, by restricting our investments to the United States we miss out on the huge opportunities available in the remainder of the world. If you went into a huge supermarket or department store that had 100 different aisles of goods or departments and were told that you could shop in only 30 of them, you probably wouldn't stand for it. Similarly by investing only in U.S. companies, we restrict our choices.

Another reason to consider investing internationally is that stock markets in several other countries have outperformed ours over the last 20 years. Notable are Hong Kong, the U.K., and Japan, although the Japanese market has languished since 1990. Furthermore, there's no really strong reason to believe that this trend won't continue. Not only does the world offer a wider range of choices for investment than are available in the United States, other parts of the world have delivered better returns to investors.

We also invest internationally because we can not only improve our returns, we can actually reduce our risk at the same time. Now isn't that the goal of every investor? By holding varying portions of our portfolio outside the United States, we can achieve both goals at the same time.

Finally, we need to consider holding a small portion of our portfolio in the emerging markets shown in the chart on page 59. These "emerging markets" constitute 77% of the world's land area and 85% of the world's population . . . but only about 25% of the world's gross domestic product (GDP).

As these markets mature and begin to produce a proportionately greater share of world GDP, the investment returns are likely to be very attractive. But don't get too heavily invested in the emerging markets. By definition they are immature by Western standards and can therefore be particularly volatile, as we saw in 1995 in Mexico.

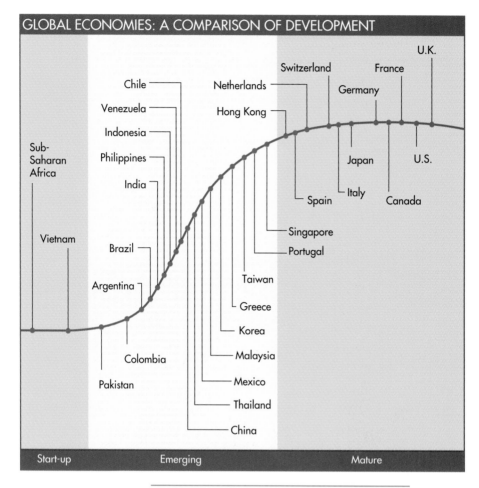

GLOBAL ECONOMIES: A COMPARISON OF DEVELOPMENT

Start-up   Emerging   Mature

KEEP AN EYE ON INTEREST RATES

There is a multitude of economic indicators used to predict the direction of the economy. Everything from housing starts to unemployment figures to car sales to the price of gold is considered. For most of us, it's really very complicated.

But here's a way to simplify the exercise by concentrating on one vital indicator: interest rates. It's not foolproof, but it can be very helpful.

Generally, high interest rates have a positive impact on savings, CDs, and Treasury bills. Conversely, high interest rates have a negative impact on businesses (borrowing costs are higher), stocks, fixed-rate bonds, and mortgage investments.

Low interest rates reverse the situation and exert a negative impact on savings, CDs, and Treasury bills, while exerting a much more positive influence on businesses (which can expand more easily on borrowing costs that are lower), stocks, and fixed-rate investments.

Using this understanding of interest rates can help us to identify investment opportunities. Let's consider the current situation.

By historical standards, interest rates are quite low today: prime is at 8.0% (at the time of writing); five-year CDs offer under 6.5%; T-bonds pay almost 7.0%; T-bills are slightly above 5.0%; and savings accounts are under 3.0%!

In keeping with our understanding of interest rates, as they have declined recently, equities have been moving ahead nicely and equity mutual funds have averaged growth of over 12% over the last three years.

Similarly, we might also want to consider investments in real estate. The real estate market in most parts of the country has improved since 1992, and it's quite likely that continued low interest rate levels will have a ripple effect—from permitting business expansion/creation to, ultimately, promoting recovery and growth in the real estate sector.

Clearly, many factors impact upon an economic cycle and determine which asset categories will experience growth. But those who pay attention to interest rate movements can often anticipate areas of future opportunity.

CHAPTER 3

Sad to say, most Americans pay more income tax than necessary—in many cases, a lot more!

As I said earlier, it's largely because they don't know the rules of the tax game, and they therefore play the game poorly. To make it even worse, many accountants and other tax preparers (to whom we often look for assistance in this regard) limit their job to calculating the amount of tax we owe, rather than educating their clients so they can plan wisely to reduce their tax burden.

We'll outline some of the best tax-saving strategies for individuals a little later, but for now, look at this example.

Which scenario would you prefer, A or B?

	A	B
Rate of return	16.0 %	16 %
Taxes (40%)	– 6.4 %	0 %
Inflation (5% average)	– 5.0 %	– 5 %
Real Rate of Return	= 4.6 %	= 11 %

Obviously you'd prefer a real rate of return of 11.0% rather than 4.6. Who wouldn't?

Coach's Quote

"Next to being shot at and missed, there's nothing quite as satisfying as a big tax refund."

Notice that, in our example, the only difference between A and B is in the amount of tax paid. How do you pay zero tax on an investment? Simple. Buy a tax-sheltered retirement program. This may be an IRA, SEP, 401(k), or Keogh, depending on your eligibility. As long as your money remains inside your account, you pay no tax on it. It grows much more rapidly, and you're getting a much better real rate of return than you would otherwise.

Note that your investment goals of growth and tax relief are not mutually exclusive. Quite the opposite—they fit beautifully together in your tax-sheltered retirement program.

EVERYBODY HAS A TAX PROBLEM

Earlier I pointed out how in 1996, 38% of the income of an average American family was paid out in taxes of all sorts. I also showed how Tax Freedom Day, the day in the year when the average American has paid all the taxes he or she owes to all levels of government, doesn't occur until May 7.

You'll also remember that tax relief is one of the three key financial objectives for Americans and that we should take advantage of tax breaks made available to us.

RETIREMENT REALITY

Retirement reality is often shockingly different from retirement dreaming or fantasizing. In the next few years, the United States will experience a dramatic increase in the number of seniors. As a result, there is no guarantee that social programs once considered universal will be continued as we know them. There is no contract with the government; programs can be wiped out, although the chances are slim; benefit postponements or reductions are more likely. With so much doubt surrounding both employer pensions and public old age security programs, growing numbers of Americans are concluding that their most reliable source of retirement will likely be their own savings programs.

It's clear, then, that saving for retirement is an absolute necessity for every American and that we cannot rely on the government to take care of us in a way that will allow us to maintain our standard of living at the level we wish.

Over and over again, statistics show that many Americans retire near or even below the poverty line. Millions of Americans, including professionals, salespeople working on commission, business owners, and employees of businesses—in fact, nearly 53% of all Americans—have neither current coverage nor prior pension plan vested benefits.[1] Retirees, in the first five years after retirement, typically discover that Social Security replaces less than 25% of their preretirement wage.[2]

Despite these scary facts, other statistics show in study after study that Americans have the naive belief that, somehow or other, the money they need in retirement will miraculously be there to allow them to live at the level to which they've become accustomed.

Remember, the reasonable goal for every American should be to retire at the income level enjoyed in his or her peak earning years.

Let's say that Jack Cooper earns a salary of $50,000 in his final year at work. How much money would he need to have saved to achieve the goal of enjoying an income of $50,000 in retirement? If we assume a 10% return on his money, you can see that he would require a nest egg of $500,000 to achieve this goal ($500,000 × 10% = $50,000.) That's a lot of money!

---

[1] U.S. Department of Labor, Pension and Welfare Benefits Administration, Office of Research and Economic Analysis, *Retirement Benefits of American Workers* (September 1995), p. 55, Table B7.

[2] Ibid., p. 91, Table D4.

Approximately 47% of American wage and salary workers contribute to pension plans,[3] some of which are very good, providing, with Social Security, up to 70% of the final year's salary.[4] But even these people need to be putting aside additional money to make up that 30% to 40% shortfall.

Again, let's take the example of Jill Bowman, who retires with retirement income (Social Security plus pension) of 65% of her final year's salary; let's assume she was earning $60,000 in that final year. Her retirement income then would be about $40,000 and she'd need to ensure an extra income of $20,000 to achieve her goal. At a 10% return on her money, she would need about $200,000 in savings ($200,000 × 10% = $20,000).

Now some will say that in retirement expenses are lower and that you don't need the same amount of income. I suppose there are some who go from work to retirement in a rocking chair, but I don't know many. My experience is that they're equally likely to travel, play golf, or get involved in a variety of sports or hobby activities—all of which cost money. Many people put off major trips until their retirement, when they'll have the time to go. But will they have the money? Don't accept the idea that you'll need less in retirement. It's not a necessary situation, but to avoid it you must plan ahead.

If all of this information about the amount of money required in retirement is depressing, let me now tell you the good news—and it is good news indeed. Not only will the government subsidize your contribution to a tax-sheltered retirement program (in some cases by nearly 40%) by allowing it as a deduction, it also allows the money to grow tax-free as long as it's in the program. Two fantastic advantages! And to make it even better, the government has recently raised retirement program contribution limits in a way that will be advantageous to thousands and thousands of Americans.

A TAX-SHELTERED RETIREMENT PROGRAM IS THE SOLUTION

There are several different types of tax-sheltered retirement programs, your choice of which may depend on the type of work you do and whom you work for. Choices include the regular IRA, the 403(b), the 401(k), the Keogh, the SEP-IRA, and the SIMPLE-IRA.

---

[3] Ibid., p. 55, Table B7.
[4] Ibid., p. 91, Table D4.

IRA

Contributions to an IRA are fully deductible if you don't have a retirement plan or if you have one and earn less than $25,000 annually (less than $40,000 if filing a joint return). The maximum contribution to an IRA is $2,000 annually per person. Husband and wife can contribute $2,000 each even though only one has earned income. Contributions to a Roth IRA are not tax deductible; withdrawals may be non-taxable.

403(b) Plans

These are available only to employees of exempt organizations and public schools. Exempt organizations include charitable and religious organizations, public schools, colleges, and universities.

Technically, the employee voluntarily reduces the amount of salary received, and the employer purchases an annuity for the employee with the amount withheld. Thus, the employee reports a smaller salary than is actually being paid, saving income taxes.

The maximum allowable annual contribution is 20% of salary up to $9,500. A further limit is that employer contributions to a retirement fund are subtracted from the $9,500 to derive the maximum contribution.

Plans for the Self-Employed

There are a variety of retirement plans that may be established by business owners and self-employed persons. One of the simplest is the SEP-IRA, to which a self-employed person may contribute up to 15% of compensation (the maximum contribution in 1997 is $24,000), which is treated as an IRA (thus requiring little administration). More complex plans include Keogh plans, SIMPLE-IRAs, and 401(k) plans. The Table on page 66 compares these plans.

401(k) Plans

When your employer has set up a 401(k), you can contribute 20% of your salary up to $9,500 per year. Contributions are tax-deferred. The employer may match or even exceed employee contributions, up to 25% of salary. The maximum combined contribution for employer and employee in 1997 is $32,000, based on $160,000 of compensation.

Table 3-1—Comparison of Retirement Plans

Lower Cost Less Administration				Higher Cost More Administration
Features	**SEP-IRA**	**KEOGH**	**SIMPLE-IRA**	**401(k)**
Eligibility	Any self-employed individual, business owner, or individual who earns any self-employed income	Any self-employed individual, business owner, or individual who earns any self-employed income	Business with 100 or fewer eligible employees	Any type of public or private company; typically used by companies with 25 or more employees
Key Advantage	Easy to set up and maintain	Highest contribution maximums	Salary reduction plan with less administration	Features such as vesting schedules and loans
Funding Responsibility	Employer contributions only	Generally, employer contributions only	Funded by employee elective deferrals and employer contributions	Primarily employee contributions and optional employer contributions
Annual Contribution Per Participant	Up to 15% of compensation, up to a maximum of $24,000 in 1997[1]	Up to 25% of compensation, up to a maximum of $32,000[1]	*Employee:* Up to $6,000 per year (indexed) *Employer: Either* match contributions up to 3% of employee's compensation up to $6,000; (can be reduced to as low as 1% in any 2 out of 5 yrs). *Or* contribute 2% of each eligible employee's compensation, up to $3,200[2]	*Employee:* Depending on plan design, could be as much as 20% of compensation, up to a maximum of $9,500 in 1997 *Employer/employee combined:* As much as 25% of compensation, up to a maximum of $32,000[1]
Access to Assets	Withdrawals at any time. Withdrawals are subject to current federal income taxes and a possible 10% penalty (if the participant is under age 59½)	Cannot take withdrawals from plan until a "trigger" event occurs. A 10% penalty may apply if you are under age 59½, or under age 55 and separated from service	Withdrawals at any time. If employee is under age 59½, withdrawals generally may be subject to a 25% penalty if taken within the first two years of beginning participation and a possible 10% penalty if taken after that time period	Cannot take withdrawals from plan until a "trigger" event occurs. May offer loan provisions and allow withdrawals in certain hardship situations (Hardship withdrawals may be subject to a possible 10% penalty if participant is under age 59½)
Vesting of Contributions	Immediate	May offer vesting schedules	Employee and employer contributions vested immediately	Employee contributions vested immediately; different vesting schedules available for employer contributions
Administrative Responsibilities/ Tax Filings	No employer tax filings	Form 5500	No employer tax filings	Form 5500 and special IRS testing to ensure plan does not discriminate in favor of highly compensated employees

Source: *Fidelity Focus*, Spring 1997, p. 14.

---

[1] For plan years beginning on or after January 1, 1997, maximum compensation on which contributions can be based is $160,000. For self-employed people, compensation means earned income.

[2] Maximum compensation on which 1997 non-elective SIMPLE-IRA contributions can be based is $160,000.

Here are three key advantages of a tax-sheltered retirement account.

Increased Contribution Limits

Starting in 1997, limits on tax-deductible IRA contributions for a married couple who do not belong to a pension plan were increased to $4,000.

Tax Savings

The total amount contributed comes directly "off the top" of your income for tax purposes and can therefore significantly reduce the amount of income tax you pay each year.

For example, if you had earned income of $40,000 in 1997, you, together with your nonworking spouse, can contribute up to $4,000 to your IRA in 1997. This means your earned income for tax purposes is $36,000. You would be approximately in the 28% tax bracket and would therefore get a tax saving in 1997 of about $1,120 (28% of $4,000). If you earned $125,000 from self-employment and filed a joint return, you could deduct more than $16,000 in a SEP-IRA and save more than $5,000. Now we're talking!

Tax-Free Growth

While the money you invest stays in the tax-sheltered retirement program (TSRP), it grows tax-free. Using the Rule of 72, we can quickly calculate that at 12% it would double in only six years. Outside the TSRP and subject to tax at 31%, your investment would take over eight years to double.

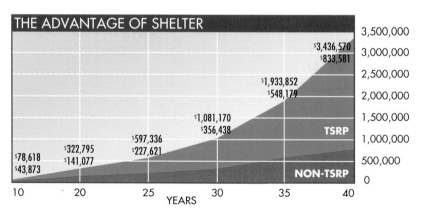

THE ADVANTAGE OF SHELTER

Assumes annual contributions of $4,000 made at the beginning of the year; 12% average annual compound rate of return; 31% combined federal-state tax rate.

START EARLY!

Diane opens an IRA that earns 12%, invests $2,000 per year for six years, and then stops. She makes no further contributions to the IRA for the next 38 years. She will end up with $1,348,440.

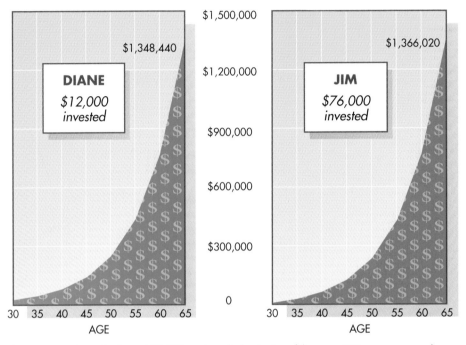

Assumes annual contributions of $2,000 made at the beginning of the year; 12% average annual compound rate of return.

Money Coach Rule

Start early and make the maximum TSRP contribution every year! Let time, compounding, and tax-free growth in a TSRP work hard for you!

Jim spends $2,000 per year for six years on himself, then opens an IRA and contributes $2,000 per year at 12% for the next 38 years. He ends up with $1,366,020.

See what happens! At age 65, Diane, who has invested only $12,000, has accumulated nearly as much as Jim, who has invested $76,000.

CONTRIBUTE EARLY IN THE YEAR OR AT LEAST MONTHLY

We've already encouraged you to use the dollar cost averaging strategy and examined the advantages of doing so. But there is another advantage in investing in your TSRP early in the year or monthly rather than in a lump sum at the end of the year. For most people, it's just easier to find a smaller amount monthly than a larger amount annually . . . usually in February when you're still facing Christmas bills.

However, the major advantage is that you'll likely earn more by investing early or monthly. The following chart sums it up very succinctly.

Does $41,000 extra make it sound attractive? It should!

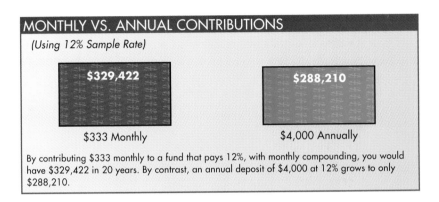

MONTHLY VS. ANNUAL CONTRIBUTIONS

(Using 12% Sample Rate)

$329,422

$288,210

$333 Monthly $4,000 Annually

By contributing $333 monthly to a fund that pays 12%, with monthly compounding, you would have $329,422 in 20 years. By contrast, an annual deposit of $4,000 at 12% grows to only $288,210.

WHERE CAN YOU INVEST YOUR TAX-SHELTERED RETIREMENT PROGRAM DOLLARS?

There is a wide range of options available for your tax-sheltered retirement program investment dollars. They include savings bonds, Treasury bills, United States government and corporate bonds, certificates of deposit (CDs), term deposits, shares listed on stock exchanges, and a growing number of mutual funds that fulfill prescribed ownership limits. There are other possibilities as well, but these are the major ones.

A regular IRA or SEP-IRA may be funded by a bank or savings and loan association or a mutual fund. Those offered by a bank or S&L are generally fixed-interest, fixed-term accounts, similar to a CD. This is what I call "loanership." You lend your money to the bank. Recently, however, as more and

Money Coach Rule

I believe that for most people a mutual fund selected to meet their investment objectives of growth, tax relief, and security should be the investment of choice because I believe that selected "ownership" will outperform "loanership" over the long term, as it has in the past.

more people have come to learn the advantages and benefits of "ownership," mutual funds have become very popular as tax-sheltered retirement account investments.

There are now thousands of mutual funds that are prepared to accept your tax-sheltered retirement program. For a regular IRA, rollover IRA, or SEP-IRA, you can choose from among nearly 10,000 mutual funds. Employees depend on programs set up by their employers for investment opportunities, and these may be more limited, sometimes offering a narrow choice of investment vehicles.

Those who work for exempt organizations generally must purchase an "annuity," which may be offered only by an insurance company. Many insurance companies, such as the huge Teachers Insurance and Annuity (TIAA) offer both fixed-income and stock (CREF) funds that are similar to mutual funds in investing habits. Lincoln Life and Variable Annuity Life Insurance Company are large insurance company players in the 403(b) market.

Mutual funds have taken over a huge share of the TSRP market. Mutual funds are a vehicle for achieving diversification and skilled management. Funds may be offered by a security salesperson, by a bank, or by the fund directly. Most funds offered through salespersons require a sales charge, called a "load," as much as 8% of the investment. In addition, all funds charge an investment management fee and incur administrative costs.

You can avoid the sales "load" by buying no-load funds. Rigorous academic studies have shown that no-load funds are managed just as well as load funds, so the investors clearly save the sales charge. The American Association of Individual Investors (AAII, 625 N. Michigan Avenue, Chicago, IL 60611) publishes an annual guide to no-load and/or low-load funds. It ranks fund performance by category (aggressive growth, growth and income, growth, bond, exempt bond, global) and offers historical data for each fund. It covers more than 800 funds.

You can reduce the ongoing expenses of your fund by buying an Index Fund. These are set up to match the performance of the Standard & Poor's (S&P) 500, S&P 100, or Dow Jones Industrial Average (DJIA). Because these need no securities analysts to try to beat the market, costs are reduced.

Find a family of funds that you believe is sound. Families include Fidelity, Vanguard, Galaxy, Putnam, Dreyfus, Franklin-Templeton, Invesco, Benham, Babson, American Century, SteinRoe, T. Rowe Price, Warburg Pincus,

Scudder, and many others. Within each family you will find funds with various investment tastes, ranging from conservative U.S. government bond funds to aggressive growth. Included are stock funds that invest for growth and income, global (international) funds, and various sector funds that invest in particular industries (banking, technology, gold, oil, etc.). Bond funds may invest in long-term or short-term bonds, U.S. government bonds, municipal bonds, corporate bonds of high quality or high income, and so on.

If you select a family of funds, you may be able to allocate your money among different funds and change the allocation in a single day with a telephone call, often without a transfer charge.

Money Coach Rule

An early start on a tax-sheltered program account is one of the best investments you can make, because it achieves all three investment goals: growth, tax relief, and security.

Morningstar, Lipper, and Kiplinger are among the prominent names that follow mutual fund performance. Data that will permit you to compare fund performance can be found in *Barron's*, *The Wall Street Journal*, *Forbes*, *Fortune*, *Business Week*, *Kiplinger's*, and *Mutual Funds Magazine*.

CONSIDER A SPOUSAL IRA

A spousal IRA is registered in the name of one spouse, but the contributions have come from the other spouse. These plans are particularly appropriate in a situation where one spouse may be at home and not earning much taxable income, and the other spouse is earning a higher income.

SPOUSE AS BENEFICIARY

An important consideration if you are married is to name your spouse as beneficiary of your IRA. If you do, the money can be transferred to your spouse's IRA on your death and remain there tax-free. If you don't name your spouse as beneficiary, the IRA will be included as an asset on your estate tax return in the year of your death, and a substantial tax bill could result. Take advantage of the unlimited marital deduction for estate tax purposes, and don't let the government get any more taxes than necessary!

THE BAD NEWS ABOUT TSRPs

I believe that TSRPs, including IRAs, which have now been in place in the United States since about 1974, are the greatest things since sliced bread!

But you know what? We're not using it nearly to full advantage.

A recent study showed that less than 50% of Americans actually have a TSRP and that we're contributing less than the maximum allowable contribution to claim a tax deduction.

It gets worse! In the moderate income range of $20,000 to $50,000, only about 22% of tax filers claimed an IRA deduction in 1986.

We've got a lot of work to do and we'd better get started fast . . . because the government simply will not be able to afford to provide the pension incomes many of us are naively expecting.

TAX-SHELTERED RETIREMENT PROGRAM REPLAY

We've seen that many of the concepts I've been urging you to use thus far are activated when you start a tax-sheltered retirement program.

- Ideally you'll begin as soon as you start earning an income.
- You'll be an owner (through purchase of mutual funds) rather than a loaner.
- You'll use the Rule of 72 to calculate the time it'll take for your investment to double and always seek the highest rate of growth (that's consistent with reasonable security).
- You'll let the magic of compounding work for you.
- You'll invest a fixed amount monthly using dollar cost averaging.
- You'll get tax relief as a result of participating in a tax-sheltered retirement program.

OTHER STRATEGIES FOR SAVING INCOME TAX

I have commented throughout the book on the importance of taxes—particularly income tax. Taxes almost invariably get in the way of our achieving the return on our investments that we'd like. That's why it's important to be aware of opportunities available to legally reduce the amount of tax we pay. That process is called tax planning; it's the minimizing of the amount we pay in income tax through the proper handling of our financial affairs.

With our government debt continuing to grow at $100 billion per year, and with no realistic likelihood of this situation drastically changing any time soon, two key trends are likely to emerge. First, government services will have to be cut.

Second, it's a virtual **certainty** that most types of taxes will rise in the future. Some predict that the marginal tax rate, now at about 28% to 39% maximum, will rise to 45% or 50%. And this doesn't include state income tax, sales tax, or property tax.

For these reasons, we must get better at tax planning . . . using every legal means available to reduce the amount we pay. Americans are strange. We pay high taxes and complain bitterly about it; but we don't actually explore all the opportunities to reduce our burden.

Tax planning involves using our knowledge of the rules, put in place by the government, to look for opportunities to reduce our taxable income. Tax-sheltered retirement programs are among the very best examples. Tax planning usually involves the assistance of a person whose judgment we trust, in whom we have confidence, and who is knowledgeable about the current tax rules . . . sounds like we're describing a money coach!

Tax planning is very different from tax evasion, which is illegal and which brings with it severe penalties including fines and possibly a jail term.

So, in addition to maximizing your tax-sheltered retirement program contributions, how else can you save taxes? While there are tax-saving opportunities available to individuals depending on their unique circumstances (e.g., business owners, the self-employed, commissioned salespeople), the following are among the favorite and best tax-saving strategies available to most Americans today.

DIVIDEND VS. INTEREST INCOME

Faced with a choice, we can save substantial income tax by electing to receive dividend or capital gains income, rather than interest income. Here's how.

Let's assume we are receiving $1,000 of investment income in the form of interest. This is what Americans often do, because they often hold a majority of their investments in cash, CDs, T-Bills, and so on, and these investments pay interest. Let's also assume for each example that you are in the 36% marginal tax bracket. In this case, as the chart shows, your $1,000 is divided so that $360 goes to the IRS and $640 comes to you. The IRS thinks that's fair; you work for the money and give them over a third! Do you think that's fair?

THE EFFECT THE "TAX MAN" HAS ON $1,000 OF INVESTMENT INCOME		
	$1,000 of Dividend or Interest Income	$1,000 of Capital Gains Income
Tax Rate @ 36%	$360	$200
After-Tax Income	$640	$800

I suggest that you invest in areas where the profits are taxed as "capital gains." Many people are under the mistaken impression that there is no tax advantage in capital gains. Wrong! After May 6, 1997, capital gains are taxed at a 20% maximum rate, whereas ordinary income can be taxed as high as 40%. In future years the capital gains rate may decline and the ordinary income rate may increase.

In our example, $1,000 of capital gains would carry a tax of $200 or less, leaving at least $800 for you, the person who earned it.

So it's important to be up to date on the tax rules as you play the "money game." It can mean extra money in your pocket.

THE "KIDDIE TAX"

If you invest money for a child under 14 in an interest-bearing investment, not only will you get comparatively low returns but you'll also be sorry to learn that the interest earned is attributable to you. You must pay tax on it at *your* tax rate! That's why CDs and bank accounts aren't great for this purpose.

A better alternative is to invest in a capital gains–seeking investment such as growth stocks. First you'll likely get much better return. But second, any capital gains can be postponed, to be realized when the child is 14 or older. The result? A smaller tax or no tax will likely be due.

CLAIM APPROPRIATE BUSINESS EXPENSES

If you are operating a small personal business, most expenses that are paid out in the course of doing business or for the purpose of developing the business can be used as deductions that may have the effect of reducing the amount of personal income tax you pay. This includes a salary that may be paid for work done by a spouse or child.

LIMITED PARTNERSHIP INVESTMENTS

These investments, sometimes called "tax shelters," allow the investor to claim tax deductions that can be applied to offset income from other sources —usually earned income. Since 1986, however, opportunities have been quite limited.

Such investments, even after the tax deductions are taken into account, sometimes require an annual out-of-pocket, after-tax expense to the investor. It's important to note that these are investments first and tax shelters second. They should be seen as such and should not be purchased primarily because they save tax.

You will have to do your homework, ask probing questions, read accompanying sales materials and legal documentation carefully, and ask for your advisor's opinion.

Limited partnerships come in many forms. In some cases, the limited partners invest in the production of movies or television series; in others they fund ventures for oil and gas or for real estate.

Traditionally, the most popular limited partnerships are land-based and range from the construction of residential townhouses or highrise apartments to commercial shopping centers or nursing homes. Limited partnerships that represent ownership in well-located and fairly priced real estate still provide excellent opportunities for growth, for tax relief, and for security. However, tax changes in 1986 made these vehicles less attractive than in the past.

Oil & Gas Limited Partnerships

For those seeking extra tax advantages, ongoing tax-favored income, and the potential for capital gain, and who at the same time wish to add a tangible asset to their portfolio, an oil and gas limited partnership investment may be appropriate.

Many people also see the addition of tangible assets such as oil and gas to a portfolio as a prudent strategy. Historically, oil and gas have acted as a hedge against inflation, rising in price when stock and bond prices decline. However, oil exploration and drilling is a high-risk venture. Think: If a promoter had certain knowledge of where oil was located, why would he want to share his discoveries and profit with you, a total stranger? So beware.

Remember Your Priorities

Don't lose sight of the priorities! Tax shelters should generally only be considered after you've paid off most or all of your mortgage, after you've made your annual tax-sheltered retirement program contribution, after you've paid off virtually all outstanding loans, after you've got a growing 10% fund, and when you're earning substantial annual income. They're not for everybody, but at the right time and for the right person, they can be very attractive investments.

ASSIGN LIMITED PARTNERSHIP INCOME TO A CHILD

If you invest in a limited partnership and receive income from it, the income will be taxed in your hands, at your marginal tax rate. This rate will presumably be near the top bracket.

One way to reduce taxes is to assign such income to a lower-tax-bracket child (age 14 or older). He or she will pay tax at his or her lower rate, resulting in what could be considerable savings. You and your spouse can each make an annual gift of the actual asset, up to $10,000 to each child every year; together that's $20,000 per year to each child or grandchild.

CONSIDER A FAMILY LIMITED PARTNERSHIP

There may be situations in which the creation of a family limited partnership is appropriate. For more information on the use of family limited partnerships, consult a knowledgeable attorney or financial planner.

YOUR MORTGAGE PAYMENTS ARE TAX DEDUCTIBLE

Assume that you have a house worth $250,000, owned free and clear of debt. You can borrow 80% of that at 8% interest with a 20-year mortgage. If you are in the 40% tax bracket, the interest cost is 4.8% after taxes. With the $200,000 you raised from the mortgage, buy tax-free municipal bonds paying 6%. You will benefit from the difference in after-tax rates, 6% compared with 4.8%. That 1.2% difference, applied to $200,000, is $2,400 per year, or $200 per month, tax-free! The tax law will allow this; in other cases, however, using borrowed money to buy tax-free bonds will result in interest expense, which is not tax-deductible.

The analysis becomes complex when everything (mortgage amortization, closing costs, risk) is considered. The main point to remember is that mortgage interest is a low-cost form of borrowing because of low interest rate availability and tax deductibility of mortgage interest. There may be attractive investment opportunities that come along. Borrowing against your house can be a low-cost way to take advantage of these opportunities.

Coach's Quote

"Paying less income tax is not the privilege of the rich; it's the plan of the wise."

KEEP UP TO DATE

These suggestions can be valuable as you try to take advantage of the income tax rules. But remember, the rules keep changing, and it's important to do your best to keep up with the changes that affect you. Metropolitan area newspapers are giving increasing attention to business and financial matters, so I suggest you read papers like *The Wall Street Journal* or the business section of your daily newspaper. In addition, a number of established business magazines are available to help inform and entertain. These include *Forbes*, *Fortune*, *Money*, and *Business Week*.

CHAPTER 4

$\int$ ecurity is definitely a vital investment objective and one that is taken seriously by virtually every investment manager.

Security is often achieved through "guarantees" offered by financial institutions that guarantee rates of interest to be paid to investors over various periods of time. The following instruments offer guarantees: certificates of deposit; U.S. savings bonds; U.S. Treasury bills, notes, and bonds; and mortgage-backed securities.

Further security is offered to Americans by the Federal Deposit Insurance Corporation (FDIC), which guarantees most deposits up to $100,000 against the default of the commercial bank or savings association that holds your funds.

But there is definitely a price to be paid for this security. For the most part, as described earlier, the price is a lower real rate of return paid by the bank or savings association. At best, you're treading water and it's probably fair to say that you'll never get rich by putting all your money in the bank.

As Americans, we traditionally have craved security and guarantees. Every year we lend millions of dollars to the government by buying savings bonds. We deposit billions of dollars with banks, savings associations, and insurance companies, and make them rich.

Of course security is important, and there is a place for "guaranteed" financial products in almost everyone's plan. But perhaps we should more often do what the banks and insurance companies do with our money once we've lent it to them at guaranteed, but comparatively low, rates of return. They invest it in securities, mortgages, and real estate, making higher rates of return, and keeping the difference for themselves, or paying for the lavish buildings they occupy, plus wages for their employees.

In this section we'll take a look at how you can build your financial defense.

• COACH'S PLAYBOOK •

Establish an emergency fund

Many financial planners and advisors suggest that you establish an emergency fund equal to about three months' salary. For many people, that's an amount in the $10,000 range. But if this amount is sitting in a savings account, it's earning low rates of interest, and the interest earned is fully taxable. I believe it's far better to use the money to pay down your mortgage, pay off consumer debt, or "top up" your IRA or other tax-sheltered retirement program.

I believe that an emergency fund is worthwhile, but I think $5,000 should generally be the maximum amount you hold in cash. It's great to have a few thousand dollars available whenever you want it. You'll no doubt sleep better at night knowing you've got money in the bank, and knowing that you can act quickly if you see a really great bargain. But don't get carried away!

The alternative I recommend is that, if you're concerned about needing cash quickly, you should establish a line of credit in an amount from $3,000 to $10,000 or more with your local bank manager.

A line of credit for $3,000 means that you can write a check or checks for up to that amount whenever you want even though you do not actually have the money in your account. You pay interest only on the amount actually used (e.g., you may write a check for $1,000 on a $3,000 line of credit; you pay interest only on the $1,000 amount). A line of credit, used effectively, can be a very valuable financial tool. Just be sure you pay it off as quickly as you can, particularly if you have used it for a consumer product, e.g., a car, stereo, trip, etc.

By establishing a line of credit, you can be sure money will be there if you need it, and, at the same time, you'll be free to invest your assets in more productive ways.

BE IT EVER SO HUMBLE, THERE'S NO PLACE LIKE HOME...ESPECIALLY IF IT'S PAID OFF

For many people, their home has been their very best investment. Depending on when they bought and what down payment they made, they've probably made a solid return of between 5% and 10% average annual compound rate on their money.

For this and several other reasons, most Americans seem to prefer home ownership.

● While it's true that there is some risk involved in the purchase of real estate, and while it's certainly not guaranteed that prices will steadily increase forever, I believe that if you choose a suitable location in an area with a diversified economy and hold your property over the long term, your home will increase in value. While no investments are "perfect," home ownership is probably in the "excellent" category.

● In addition to a reasonable rate of return, your principal residence might be tax free on sale, which means that the real rate of return (average annual rate minus taxes—in this case, zero—minus inflation) is likely to be somewhere around 3% to 8%, which is excellent. There is no tax on a sale after May 6, 1997, provided that you owned and occupied the home as a principal residence for two of the five years prior to the sale. Up to $250,000 of gain per person can be excluded ($500,000 for a married couple if both qualify).

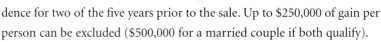

You remember earlier I said that anything above a 3% real rate of return is outstanding. Because all the growth is tax-free, some people accurately consider their home to be the ultimate tax shelter.

● As well, the home symbolizes many of the true joys of life: children born and raised, happy holiday memories around a fireplace or by the pool. A home is far more than an investment; it's a way of life to the extent that many people don't even consider their home as anything other than a home. For most, even though they don't recognize it, it's far more than a place to live, and the phrase "joy of owning your own home" has more than one meaning.

Coach's Quote

"If you think nobody cares if you're alive, try missing a couple of mortgage payments."

● My grandfather used to say that the best way to save is to be forced to—through debt. Most people who buy a home today have some debt on it in the form of a mortgage. And most take their mortgage payments seriously (or they should). Thus a home can be seen as the ultimate in forced savings. Bit by bit the mortgage is paid off, and, ultimately, we not only own the home outright, but are delighted to discover that it's worth far more than it was when we bought it!

It's clear that there are many good reasons for purchasing if possible. But even if you do not purchase a home, it's not the end of the world! Certainly the place you live can be a center of years of happy family activity whether it's rented or owned. And don't forget that this ideal of home ownership is primarily a North American phenomenon. Millions and millions of people throughout the world rent rather than own their home or apartment and are content doing so.

But if we look at the owned home as a good investment, how can a renter achieve similar growth? Let's assume that Don can rent an apartment for $1,000 a month or buy it for $1,350 a month in mortgage costs—the difference is $350 per month. If Don rented all his life and invested the $350 (in addition to his 10% fund), he'd be in a very healthy financial condition. Remember the power of compounding over the long term? The difficulty might be that while he'd be forced to make the $1,350 payment monthly or lose the apartment, he might not be disciplined enough to set that extra $350 per month aside for 20 or 25 years.

In addition, interest expenses and property taxes are deductible expenses on your tax return. Let us suppose that, of the $1,350 monthly payment, $800 is interest and $300 is for property taxes. (The rest of the payment is for insurance and principal reduction.) This allows $1,100 of the monthly payment to be tax-deductible. For someone in the 33% tax bracket (28% federal plus 5% state), the monthly after-tax cost is $987, which is less than the cost of renting, as shown below:

Monthly payment		$1,350
Less interest	$800	
Property taxes	300	
	$1,100	
Tax rate	× .33	
Income tax savings		363
After-tax cost		$987

According to the Home Price Index published by the Office of Federal Housing Enterprise Oversight, home ownership in the United States has proved to be an excellent investment. The index value, which began at 102.09 in 1980, climbed in every single year through 1995, the most current year available, when it reached 192.08. The index is a measure of home prices that looks at the resale of the same home in two different periods. By using home resales only, the index overcomes flaws of other indexes of housing prices. Other indexes that measure average or median housing prices are affected by

Money Coach Rule

Buy your own home if at all possible. The joy of home ownership, the tax-free position on sale, the traditionally good rate of return on real estate, plus the fact that it's an excellent form of forced saving all make home ownership a very attractive goal for just about anyone.

changing characteristics of houses sold from one year to the next. The OFHEO's index also reflects the effect of wear and tear on a home as it ages.

Generally, housing prices keep up with inflation. In many areas where land is scarce and development pressures are great, housing prices have advanced at a pace well beyond the rate of inflation.

PAY DOWN THE MORTGAGE FAST: HERE'S HOW

If you buy a home and have a mortgage, it probably represents your single biggest monthly commitment. It is also paid completely in after-tax dollars. ("After-tax dollars" means that every dollar paid off against your mortgage has already been taxed. So depending on your tax rate, you have to earn between $1.18 and $1.75 to pay off every dollar of your mortgage.) That's painful, and it's one reason to pay off your mortgage as quickly as you can.

The second reason you should pay off your mortgage fast is that it costs you a tremendous amount of interest when you have a mortgage. Did you know that if you pay off your mortgage over 30 years at 9%, you will have paid not only the original amount you borrowed but also almost twice that amount in interest? Shocking but true!

The accompanying chart shows that at 9% over 30 years, it costs $227,400 to borrow $120,000! If you are fortunate, interest rates will be lower when you borrow, but we still pay huge amounts of interest when we take a mortgage.

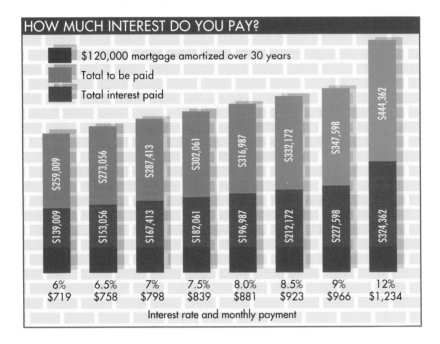

HOW MUCH INTEREST DO YOU PAY?

- $120,000 mortgage amortized over 30 years
- Total to be paid
- Total interest paid

	6% $719	6.5% $758	7% $798	7.5% $839	8.0% $881	8.5% $923	9% $966	12% $1,234
Total to be paid	$259,009	$273,056	$287,413	$302,061	$316,987	$332,172	$347,598	$444,362
Total interest paid	$139,009	$153,056	$167,413	$182,061	$196,987	$212,172	$227,598	$324,362

Interest rate and monthly payment

As an introduction to this topic of mortgages, it's important to understand a key term, amortization.

The amortization period is the length of time it will take the mortgage to be completely paid off. The shorter the amortization period, the sooner the mortgage will be paid off.

Let's say you borrow $120,000 to buy a home (i.e., you take a $120,000 mortgage) at 9% with a 30-year amortization.

It would cost $965.55 per month for 30 years to fully amortize the debt. Amortization is not linear: in the early years, very little of the mortgage payment goes toward principal reduction; most goes toward interest. In the last few years, most of the payment goes toward principal.

• COACH'S PLAYBOOK •

Four great ways to pay off your mortgage fast

Now, let's look at four ways to pay off your mortgage as quickly as possible.

1. Reduce amortization period

Let's go back to the example we used earlier: A $120,000 mortgage at 9% costs $965.55 per month and amortized (paid off) in 30 years. Examine the chart on the left and note that over the 30-year life of the mortgage, the home-owner/borrower will pay a total of $347,598. Of that, $120,000 is the repayment of the principal, the rest is interest paid in after-tax dollars.

Now look at what happens if the borrower decides to take a 20-year amortization period. The monthly payments will increase by about only $114, but the debt will be paid off 10 years earlier, and he would have paid back $259,121—a savings of over $88,000! If we really push to reduce the amortization period to 15 years, we pay $1,217.12 per month, or a total of $219,081 and save over $128,000 compared with the cost of a 30-year amortization.

When shopping for a mortgage, then, pay as much as you can afford monthly in order to obtain the shortest amortization period possible. You'll save thousands of dollars.

2. Make "double-up payments" whenever possible

The chart on page 83 shows the value of making two "extra" monthly payments a year, i.e., making 14 payments a year rather than 12.

Slash your mortgage payments!

How reducing amortization period can cut your total mortgage payment by thousands of dollars.

	A	B	C
Mortgage amount	$120,000	$120,000	$120,000
Amortization	30 Years	20 Years	15 Years
Interest rate	9%	9%	9%
Monthly payment	965.55	1,079.67	1,217.12
Annual payment	11,586.60	12,956.04	14,605.44
Payment over the life of the mortgage	$347,598.00	$259,120.80	$219,081.60
B & C reduce their costs by		$88,477.20	$128,516.40

Notice that the amount of interest saved by doing so is over $106,000. The result is that the mortgage will be paid off more than 12 years earlier than would otherwise have been the case. In effect, the amortization period has been reduced, and more than $100,000 has been saved because the "double-up payments" serve to reduce the principal owed and therefore reduce the interest paid, too.

Save on mortgage interest!

How "doubling up" mortgage payments twice a year can cut mortgage interest by 46%!

	Regular mortgage (30 years @9%)	2 double-up payments per year
Mortgage principal	$120,000	$120,000
		$121,594
Interest paid	$227,598	$106,004 (46%)
Interest saved		
Years until mortgage paid off	30 years	17 years, 10 months

3. Make weekly rather than monthly payments

The advantage here is similar to making double-up payments. When you pay monthly, there are 12 cycles in the year. But by paying weekly, you add a cycle (i.e., 52 weeks/4 = 13 cycles). This extra "cycle" really constitutes a "double-up payment" and has the effect of reducing the amortization period and therefore the amount of money actually paid.

4. Make lump sum payments

Many banks, savings associations, or mortgage companies that offer mortgages now allow the option of making an annual lump sum payment of 20% of the original mortgage amount. If you borrowed $120,000 originally, you would be allowed to pay up to $24,000 against the principal amount annually—often on a date of your choice.

Again the effect is to reduce the amortization period, reduce the total amount of interest you pay by thousands of dollars, and thus free your capital for other investments or important family or personal projects.

TSRP OR MORTGAGE PAYDOWN?

People often ask me whether they should contribute to their TSRP or pay down their mortgage.

The answer is yes—to both questions. Here's how I suggest they do it.

Make your maximum annual TSRP contribution if at all possible. One reason, of course, is to get a tax break, but the other factor is time. The longer your money is invested tax-free, the larger the amount it will become. Don't wait to start your TSRP until you've paid off your mortgage—start now!

Then, take the tax savings you get from your TSRP contribution and use it to pay down your mortgage. If you contribute $4,000 to your and your spouse's IRAs and get a $1,120 tax refund, put that against your mortgage. The rule of thumb is that by every dollar you reduce your mortgage by, you save between $3 and $4 in interest payments over the life of the mortgage.

If you use this strategy every year, you can effectively build your TSRP and significantly reduce your mortgage at the same time.

LIFE INSURANCE: BUY TERM AND INVEST THE DIFFERENCE

It's probably fair to say that most people should have life insurance coverage equal to about five to 10 times their salary. Americans average about three to four times their salary. Part of the reason is that we continue to buy a more expensive type of insurance than is necessary and can't afford the right amount of coverage. This is a major problem, because life insurance is one of the most important purchases a family makes. It's therefore critical to make the right decision.

WHAT'S THE PURPOSE OF LIFE INSURANCE?

Life insurance is not really "life insurance" at all! It's probably better to call it "income replacement insurance" or "financial protection for dependents." If you were to die tomorrow, your life insurance should replace your income for your dependents. But there's more to it than that!

HOW MUCH DO I NEED?

The answer probably is "More than you think!" There are several things that insurance should do for your heirs:

Coach's Quote

"Lack of money is the root of all evil." — Mark Twain

It Should Replace Your Income

We have a habit of living to the level of our income. If you earned $50,000 at the time of your death, you will ideally have provided the means by which your family could continue to enjoy a $50,000 income after your death. How do you do this?

The simple answer is to say that you require 10 times the level of your current income in life insurance to ensure this level, that is, $50,000 income × 10 = $500,000 life insurance invested at 10% = $50,000. Of course, many people have term insurance coverage at work of up to three to five times their salary, and this should be a factor in deciding how much additional coverage is required. The truth is that while a 10% return is not impossible, the proceeds from a life insurance policy would probably be placed in a very conservative investment such as a bank CD. So a 5% return may be more realistic. This means you would need $1 million in coverage to ensure a $50,000 income in perpetuity for your heirs.

It Should Consider the Surviving Spouse's No. 1 Enemy: Inflation

An insurance policy that provides a $50,000 income in year 1 is great! But, several years later, that $50,000 is significantly reduced in terms of purchasing

power. That may put tremendous pressure on a family, especially if it means that an untrained spouse is forced to return to the work force. Even then, it may not be enough to keep the family afloat.

It's true many people may be prepared to return to work after the death of a spouse. While this may reduce the amount of insurance required to replace income, a general rule of thumb is that one should consider life insurance coverage ranging between five and 10 times the current gross income!

Inflation's effect on reducing purchasing power is the flip side of the power of compounding on savings. It must be considered in determining how much insurance is required, and it may require the purchase of up to an additional $100,000 or more of life insurance.

It Should Pay Off All Debt

This includes your mortgage and any other debt you may have, including car loans, bank loans, and so on. The last thing a grieving spouse needs at the time of death is to be burdened with debt of any kind. The implication here is that both spouses should be covered to a level that will pay off all debt.

It Should Cover Future Obligations

These obligations would probably include immediate funeral expenses up to $15,000, current day-care expenses (if applicable), and longer-term university or college expenses. While you probably expect (as I do) that the student should cover at least some expenses, a sum for assistance should be incorporated here.

THE THEORY OF DECREASING RESPONSIBILITY

One of the most common misunderstandings about life insurance is a belief that it is a permanent need of families. This is not true! Life insurance is a means of "buying time" until you get your financial house in order. You need more coverage when you're younger—less when you're older.

When your responsibilities are greatest, that is, when you're young and have children and a mortgage, your insurance needs are greatest. As you age, your payments and mortgage are reduced until you reach the point of owning your home outright. This is the time when your death protection needs (in the form of insurance) are reduced and you can instead focus on accumulating cash for your retirement years.

YOUR INSURANCE NEEDS

Early in life you require more coverage...	Later in life you require less coverage...
1. Debts are many (e.g., mortgage, car) 2. Children are young 3. Loss of income would cause family suffering	1. Few debts (e.g., no mortgage) 2. Children are grown 3. Saving for retirement
Few assets Many obligations	Many assets Few obligations

For a discussion of the important role insurance can play in estate planning see Chapter 6.

WHAT KIND OF INSURANCE SHOULD I BUY?

You should buy low-cost, no-frills term insurance rather than more expensive whole life insurance and invest the difference between the cost of the two in a promising investment program. Specifically, I recommend you be the owner of one or more mutual funds either inside or outside a tax-sheltered retirement program.

WHAT'S TERM INSURANCE?

Term insurance is a simple low-cost insurance that has only one provision: If you die, your heirs will receive a stipulated amount of money. Period. In a sense, it's similar to home or car insurance. You want protection to a certain level for a certain period, as cheaply as you can get it! You'd laugh if someone suggested that a savings or investment program should be part of your car or home insurance coverage.

WHAT'S WHOLE LIFE INSURANCE?

Whole life insurance offers a promise to pay a fixed amount (face value) on death combined with an investment or savings or "cash value" program that often pays only 3% to 5%! But when you die, your beneficiary receives only the face value; the cash value stays with the insurance company. Can you believe it? This combination of features is called the "bundling concept."

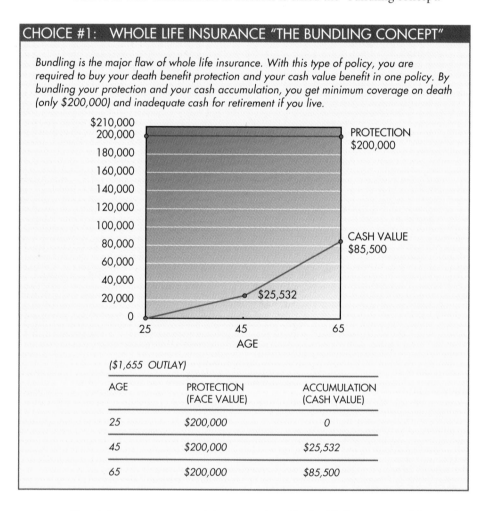

CHOICE #1:   WHOLE LIFE INSURANCE "THE BUNDLING CONCEPT"

Bundling is the major flaw of whole life insurance. With this type of policy, you are required to buy your death benefit protection and your cash value benefit in one policy. By bundling your protection and your cash accumulation, you get minimum coverage on death (only $200,000) and inadequate cash for retirement if you live.

($1,655 OUTLAY)

AGE	PROTECTION (FACE VALUE)	ACCUMULATION (CASH VALUE)
25	$200,000	0
45	$200,000	$25,532
65	$200,000	$85,500

Now let me suggest a much better option: Choice #2. Buy term and invest the difference in a tax-sheltered retirement program!

CHOICE #2: BUY THE RIGHT KIND OF LIFE INSURANCE

Buy term (age 25)

Whole Life
(Guaranteed level premium/
non-participating)
$200,000 coverage
Annual premium $1,655

Term
(Ten-year renewable term)

$200,000 coverage
Initial premium $275

... and invest the difference

Cash value after 20 years
(age 45) = **$25,532**
Cash value after 40 years
(age 65) = **$85,500**

**Difference in annual premiums
invested for**

	20 years (age 45)[1]	40 years (age 65)[2]
at 5%	$47,913	$127,127
at 6%	$53,810	$172,576
at 10%	$86,943	$584,909
at 12%	$111,364	$1,074,250
at 15%	$162,578	$2,660,839

Which would you prefer?[3]

Note: Rates for choices 1 & 2 are based on 1997 rates of a leading U.S. insurance company. Rates and benefits vary by company.

[1] Based on the future value of an annuity in advance of $1,380 per year for 20 years ($1,655 – 275 = $1,380).

[2] Based on reinvesting the sum received after 20 years for an additional 20 years.

[3] In this illustration, the whole life policy will continue in force to age 65, and beyond, for the same premium, $1,655 per year. The cost of term insurance will rise significantly with age but is likely to remain well below the cost of whole life insurance for many years. The savings on term insurance (if any) after 20 years has not been added to the column at age 65.

INSURANCE REPLAY

Follow these rules/coaching tips for buying life insurance:

● Buy only low-cost term insurance. Compare the rates of several companies that offer term insurance and buy the least expensive policy you can find.

● Buy adequate coverage. While circumstances are different for everyone, a general rule of thumb is to hold coverage of between five and 10 times your current income.

- Compare the cost of term and whole life coverage—buy term and invest the difference. Be an owner and not a loaner, i.e., buy mutual funds— don't lend your money to a bank/trust company.

- Use insurance as an estate-planning tool.

- Singles and children generally require only enough insurance to cover burial costs. Singles who don't have dependents don't require income replacement.

- Children generally don't require anything more than burial expenses.

- Stay away from fancy and costly insurance options. Don't "load up" with accidental death, option to purchase additional insurance, child riders, etc.

- Mortgage insurance is nothing more than life insurance. Don't have a separate mortgage insurance policy; rather, increase the level of life coverage on both spouses. The same is true of short-term debt, i.e., bank and car loans, etc. It tends to be much more expensive to insure these loans than to buy additional life insurance.

CHAPTER 5

ENRICH YOUR RETIREMENT

G one are the days when, at age 65 with the obligatory company watch in hand, the retiree finds his rocking chair, lights up his pipe, and withdraws from life.

One mistake many Americans make in planning for retirement is their assumption that "retirement" is a period far in the future. They figure that when they retire, they will be "old," having little remaining time, and perhaps little desire, to live. Nothing could be farther from the truth! With advances in medicine and improvements in living conditions, the average expected life span for Americans continues to increase. At the same time, although some Americans are extending their working life, many nowadays are retiring at a much younger age than their parents did.

So today's retirees are often younger, healthier, more involved in a variety of sports or activities, and more determined not to withdraw from life. Today's retirees also have plans to travel, perhaps extensively, and recognize that their involvements and interests can be comparatively expensive.

Retirees also recognize that they have one-quarter to one-third of their life ahead of them. In many cases, particularly if they have a solid pension, today's retirees will be in the same tax bracket as they were when they were earning a salary! For all those reasons, while security will be a higher priority than it was earlier, one cannot ignore the other objectives of growth and tax relief! You can't finance one-quarter to one-third of your life if inflation is devouring your purchasing power.

Early retirement is due in part to pressures from the work force. Many large companies, in order to downsize, have offered attractive incentives for early retirement. But you should also realize that there are many situations in which, from a tax standpoint, you have effectively "retired." In such situations, you receive, perhaps unexpectedly, a large lump-sum distribution of funds that had been invested in a pension or profit-sharing plan. This can happen at any age when you leave a job (whether you are terminated or quit), or when your employer ends a pension or profit-sharing plan or permanently stops making payments to it, and you receive your complete share.

When this happens, you may have as few as 60 days to decide what to do with this windfall. For this reason, you should start planning now for such an eventuality, whether it happens at age 59 ½, age 65 or 70, or next week.

There are two sure-fire ways to achieve growth, tax relief, and security at retirement. One is to "roll over" your tax-sheltered retirement plan, or a lump-sum retirement allowance, into an IRA. The other is to leave all your retirement plans in place as long as possible.

1. ROLL YOUR LUMP-SUM RETIREMENT ALLOWANCE INTO AN IRA

Many people receive a lump-sum payment called a "lump-sum retirement allowance" at the time of retirement. This amount is eligible to be "rolled over" into an IRA within 60 days of receiving the distribution, and in most circumstances should be.

If you do place it in an IRA, you do not pay tax on it (which would be up to nearly 40% of the payment!), and it can continue to grow and compound tax-free until you take it out. As we'll see in a moment, all of it can remain in your IRA until you are 71.

Let's say you retire at 59, that you receive a lump-sum retirement allowance of $40,000, and that you invest it and receive a 12% average annual return on the money. What will the $40,000 grow to by the time you turn 71? Well, the Rule of 72 tells us that at 12%, it would double in six years (72 ÷ 12 = 6). Therefore, it will grow to $80,000 when you're 65 (59 + 6), and to $160,000 by the time you turn 71 (65 + 6)!

You can be somewhat conservative and still get 12%. Thus, by rolling over your retirement allowance into an IRA, you can still get growth (from $40,000 to $160,000), tax relief (you achieve tax-free growth within an IRA), and security (through conservative investment).

You can roll over into an IRA in many situations other than retirement, including these:

1. Upon leaving your job, whether you are terminated or quit.

2. When you are age 59½ or older.

3. When your employer ends a pension or profit-sharing plan or permanently stops making payments to it, and you receive your complete share.

4. When you receive a distribution as part of a divorce or separation agreement.

5. Upon your spouse's death if you are the beneficiary of a retirement plan (does not apply to a death benefit exclusion).

Rollover Options from Employer Plans

There are choices to be made when considering a lump-sum distribution, and these may be complicated. You may have only 60 days to make a crucial decision. If you are in doubt, I suggest that you open a new IRA. Rather than commingle your distribution with an existing IRA, open a new one so that these funds retain the IRA option while you take longer to make a decision. (The option is that a new employer may accept your funds into its plan.) Be careful to select for this purpose an IRA that has minimal entry and termination fees so that, if you change your mind, this decision is not costly.

60-day rule. Employer-plan rollovers to an IRA must take place within 60 days of the date the distribution is made to you. This may be awkward in an unexpected employment termination situation, as you may need the money for living costs and you don't have time to study your options. In addition, the employer may have withheld 20% for income tax purposes. You will have to make up that 20% shortfall from your own funds, or else the amount will be treated as a taxable distribution, possibly with an early withdrawal penalty.

Self-employment ends. If you stop being self-employed, your money must remain in your IRA or Keogh plan until age 59½. An early distribution results in a 10% penalty plus the tax. One exception is that if you become permanently disabled, even before age 59½, you can avoid the penalty (but you must pay the tax).

Rollovers upon Retirement

You may be given an option at retirement to stay in the company's retirement plan and receive a monthly check or to receive a lump-sum retirement allowance, which can be rolled over into an IRA.

If you accept a distribution from the employer's plan, taxes may be more favorable (than from an IRA) because part of the distribution may be taxed at long-term capital gains rates. In addition, some distributions are eligible for a favorable averaging rule.

If you roll the lump sum over into an IRA, you have a greater choice of and control over the investment vehicle. In addition, the rollover funds continue to build up, tax-free, in the IRA. This may overcome the tax disadvantage of a distribution from an IRA.

For many people, the choice depends on what you want to do. Many people prefer to receive the distribution, pay a tax, and enjoy the good things in life that were previously unaffordable. As travel agents say, "If you don't go first class when you can afford to, your heirs will." For those who find it hard to save, a monthly pension check may be the best option. For those advised by financial planners, an IRA rollover is preferred.

The tax implications of taking a lump sum without a rollover are harsh because you must pay the tax up front. Capital gains treatment and averaging may soften the bite, however. As a compromise, you can also use an IRA rollover to defer a part of the distribution and pay the tax on the balance not rolled over.

If you are underage (59½ for IRA distributions, 55 for qualified plan distributions), you also face a 10% penalty for early withdrawal. Moreover, if the combined value of your lump-sum distribution exceeds $750,000, you may have to deal with a 15% excise tax.

Company Pension Plans Continuation

Many American employees are covered by a defined-benefit pension plan. At retirement, the monthly payment is determined by the number of years of service and salary at retirement (or the salary averaged over the three or five years preceding retirement). Some plans offer a lump-sum alternative to a monthly entitlement, which may be rolled over as described earlier.

The type of annuity payment offered may vary. These include *single-life, joint-and-last-survivor,* and *fixed-term* annuities. These are described later in the section on annuities.

2. LEAVE YOUR IRAs IN PLACE AS LONG AS YOU CAN

It's important to leave your tax-sheltered retirement program in place as long as possible to allow the greatest amount of tax-free compounding that you can achieve and to defer paying taxes as long as possible. Current rules allow you to continue to hold an IRA until April 1 of the year following the year in which you turn 70½.

Money Coach Rule

You simply cannot afford to ignore the importance of growth and tax relief as investment objectives even after you retire. If you do, it's at your peril!

To do this, of course, the corollary is that you will live on Social Security, pension income, or other earned income. You may wish to continue to work part-time or on a consulting basis. These activities will generate earned income and, ideally, will allow you to leave your tax-sheltered retirement programs undisturbed for the longest possible time, that is, until age 71.

If it is not possible to leave your retirement programs untouched until age 71, it's comforting to know that if you hold them in mutual funds you can easily arrange a periodic withdrawal program that meets your needs. Note that this is not generally true with CDs, which are "locked in" for a predetermined period of time, and it's another reason why I recommend the flexibility of mutual funds. It's important to remember that whenever you withdraw money from a retirement program, you pay tax on it, at your then-current marginal rate of tax. If you are under age 59½, you will also pay a penalty of 10%. The penalty is waived, as of 1997, if it is used to pay medical expenses in excess of 7½% of adjusted gross income.

A last quick word on inflation . . . it never retires! Historically, inflation has chewed away at our earning power at the rate of about 3% to 5% per year. Put another way, earnings must increase by at least 5% just to stay even.

You may have just retired and have an annual income of $40,000 in retirement. You've likely got another 20 to 25 years to live. Look at the accompanying chart and note how much your annual income will have to be in 20 to 25 years just to keep up with inflation. I'll bet you're shocked at the figure!

INFLATION AT 5% MEANS TROUBLE

PRESENT INCOME	10 YEARS	15 YEARS	20 YEARS	25 YEARS
$20,000	$32,578	$41,579	$53,066	$67,727
$25,000	$40,722	$51,973	$66,332	$84,659
$30,000	$48,867	$62,368	$79,599	$101,591
$35,000	$57,011	$72,762	$92,865	$118,522
$40,000	$65,156	$83,157	$106,132	$135,454
$45,000	$73,300	$93,552	$119,398	$152,386
$50,000	$81,445	$103,946	$132,665	$169,318
$55,000	$89,589	$114,341	$145,931	$186,250
$60,000	$97,734	$124,736	$159,198	$203,181

The chart above shows how much your income must grow just to meet the effects of 5% inflation. For example, today's $60,000 must grow to $203,181 in 25 years just to stay even with the higher cost of living brought on by inflation.

Remember too, you'll likely be paying tax on all your income.

HERE'S HOW TO ACHIEVE GROWTH, TAX RELIEF, AND SECURITY AFTER AGE 71

Under current legislation, you must begin receiving distributions from your IRAs beginning April 1 of the year following the year in which you turn 70½. What happens to your money then? You have essentially three options:

1. You can withdraw some or all of it and pay tax on it at that time.

2. If you don't withdraw it, you will pay a tax of 50% of the amount that should have been withdrawn.

3. You can buy an annuity.

The severe penalty of option 2 and the low rate of return offered by annuities in option 3 render option 1 the only viable option.

WHAT IS AN ANNUITY?

An annuity is simply a contract with an insurance company or other financial institution that promises you fixed, periodic payments for a set period in return for an initial lump-sum investment you make. When you buy an annuity you are essentially buying a stream of income.

Your investment decision is limited to the initial purchase, that is, when to buy, what type to buy, and from whom to buy. Beyond those initial decisions, you have little flexibility to change your mind or the nature of your assets.

Annuities can be purchased from insurance companies. Generally, your income is determined at the time of purchase, depending on the level of interest rates in the market at that time, and you are usually locked in to that rate. This, of course, is attractive if you buy at a time when rates are higher than normal, and much less attractive if you buy when rates are uncharacteristically low. As a general rule of thumb, you can buy a monthly income stream that is approximately 1% of the funds used to buy it, that is, a $100,000 annuity offers approximately $1,000 per month.

BASIC TYPES OF ANNUITY

There are three basic types of annuity:

I. LIFE ANNUITY

A life annuity pays the highest annual income for life, but payments cease entirely upon your death. If there are any assets remaining at the time of your death, they are kept by the insurance company. In theory, it's possible for one to purchase a $100,000 annuity, receive one $1,000 payment, and then die. The remaining $99,000 would remain the property of the insurance company. Under this plan there would be no provision for any of the money to go to one's spouse or family.

One way to avoid such an extreme situation is to purchase a life annuity with a guaranteed term. The guaranteed term can be as short as five years or as long as the amount of time it takes you to reach age 90.

Let's assume one purchased a plan like this with a 10-year guaranteed period and died in year six. The spouse or beneficiary would continue to receive payments for four more years. If at that time there are remaining assets, they remain the property of the insurance company. Note, too, that for every "extra" attached to this annuity, including the guaranteed period, the monthly income is reduced. (If you outlive the guaranteed period, you will continue to receive payments for the rest of your life—it is a life annuity.)

2. JOINT-AND-LAST-SURVIVOR LIFE ANNUITY

This type of annuity makes payments on the lives of two people, ensuring payments until the death of the last surviving spouse, and can be valuable in providing peace of mind that your spouse would be guaranteed a certain level of income even after your death.

This annuity can also be bought with a guaranteed term, and it is possible to arrange lower payments to the survivor after the death of a spouse. These can be 25% or 50% lower on the assumption that it costs less for one to live than two.

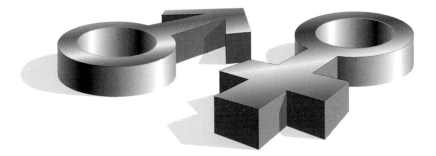

Again, the "extras" built into the plan will affect the monthly income received. In the situation described above, when the survivor accepts a lower payment on the death of a spouse, there would be slightly higher income when both were alive. But even here, the estate would receive nothing following the death of the last surviving spouse unless there was a guaranteed period attached to the annuity and it had not expired.

3. FIXED-TERM ANNUITY

This type provides payments for a fixed period of time—specifically until you or your spouse reach age 90. There are no further payments regardless of how long you live.

However, this annuity allows for your estate to receive any remaining payments after the death of both spouses if both deaths occur before age 90—the end of the fixed term. The remaining money would be taxed as a total before being paid to the estate. In this respect, this annuity is different from the others mentioned above, which do not allow benefits to heirs; on the other hand, income ceases at age 90.

ANNUITIES IN SUMMARY

Overall, annuities tend to be less flexible than many people would like and certainly less flexible than a wisely selected IRA.

When you purchase an annuity, you essentially turn your money over to an insurance company, and you give up any future control over the funds. In return, you are promised an annual income. This income is usually fixed and therefore is eroded by inflation, although some annuities have now begun to introduce an inflation factor. When this is part of an annuity, a lower starting annual income almost invariably results.

A COMBINATION OF IRAs AND ANNUITIES

Review the accompanying table and select the options best suited to meet your needs. While I believe an IRA most effectively meets the basic investment objectives of growth, tax relief, and security, it is true that for some

RETIREMENT INCOME OPTIONS

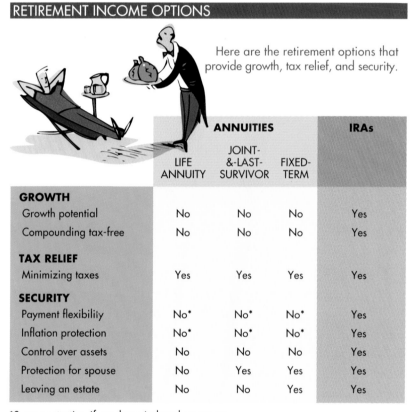

Here are the retirement options that provide growth, tax relief, and security.

	ANNUITIES			IRAs
	LIFE ANNUITY	JOINT-&-LAST-SURVIVOR	FIXED-TERM	
GROWTH				
Growth potential	No	No	No	Yes
Compounding tax-free	No	No	No	Yes
TAX RELIEF				
Minimizing taxes	Yes	Yes	Yes	Yes
SECURITY				
Payment flexibility	No*	No*	No*	Yes
Inflation protection	No*	No*	No*	Yes
Control over assets	No	No	No	Yes
Protection for spouse	No	Yes	Yes	Yes
Leaving an estate	No	No	Yes	Yes

*Some protection if you have indexed payments.

people certain aspects of an annuity may be particularly appealing. For example, for someone concerned about caring for a spouse until death regardless of age, a joint-and-last-survivor annuity may be appropriate.

These are critical decisions, and it's important to consult with your professional advisor, who will be able to assist you in making the right decision and selecting the right option or options for you. Fortunately, it doesn't have to be either an IRA or an annuity.

REVERSE MORTGAGE

Another option that is becoming increasingly popular with retired people is the reverse mortgage. This allows people in retirement to draw on the equity that has been built up in their home over the years. It is especially useful for people who are house rich and cash poor.

The Department of Housing and Urban Development (HUD) offers a reverse mortgage called the Home Equity Conversion Mortgage (HECM). Here's how it works. First, the home is debt-free or the balance owed is small. The borrowers must be at least age 62 and agree to accept mortgage counseling. A mortgage is taken out on the home. The owner has three basic payment options:

1. *Tenure payment.* The borrower receives monthly payments from the lender for as long as the borrower occupies the home as a principal residence.

2. *Term payment.* The borrower receives monthly payments for a fixed period of time, selected by the borrower.

3. *Line of credit payment.* The borrower can make draws up to a maximum amount at any time and in amounts of the borrower's choosing.

All borrowers must be counseled by a HUD-approved counseling agency. Counseling covers the reverse mortgage concept and alternatives to the reverse mortgage.

Unlike ordinary home equity loans, a HUD reverse mortgage does not require repayment as long as the borrower lives in the home. Lenders recover their principal, plus interest, when the home is sold. The remaining value of the home goes to the homeowner or to his or her survivors. If the sales proceeds are insufficient to pay the amount owed, HUD will pay the lender the amount of the shortfall. The Federal Housing Administration, which is part of HUD, collects an insurance premium from all borrowers to provide this coverage.

For example, based on a loan at an interest rate of approximately 9%, a 65-year-old could borrow up to 26% of the home's value, a 75-year-old could borrow up to 39%, and an 85-year-old could borrow up to 56%.

There are no asset or income limitations on borrowers receiving HUD's reverse mortgages.

There are also no limits on the value of homes qualifying for a HUD reverse mortgage. However, the amount that may be borrowed is capped by the maximum FHA mortgage limit for the area, which varies from $78,660 to $155,220, depending on local housing costs. As a result, owners of high-priced homes can't borrow any more than owners of homes valued at the FHA limit.

FHA's reverse mortgage insurance may make HUD's program less expensive to borrowers than the smaller reverse mortgage programs run by private lenders without FHA insurance.

For further information on the Home Equity Conversion Mortgage (HECM), contact:

U.S. Department of Housing and Urban Development
251 Cumberland Bend Drive, Suite 200
Nashville, TN 37228-1803
(615) 736-5786

As an example of use of a reverse mortgage, suppose that a homeowner is age 75, with a house valued at $128,200. The homeowner can borrow $50,000 in cash, which is 39% of its value. There are no asset or income limits on the borrower.

Suppose further that the interest rate is 9%, while the home is rising in value by 5% per year. At that rate, after 10 years, the house will be worth approximately $209,000 and the mortgage, with interest that has accrued but not been paid, will have increased to approximately $122,600. At that time, based on these assumptions, there will still be more than $86,000 of equity

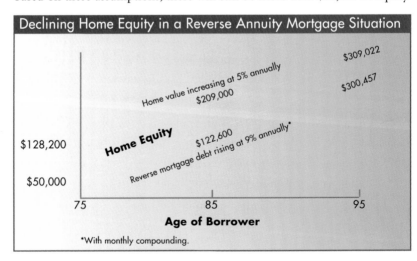

Declining Home Equity in a Reverse Annuity Mortgage Situation

Home value increasing at 5% annually
$309,022
$300,457
$209,000

Home Equity

$122,600
Reverse mortgage debt rising at 9% annually*

$128,200

$50,000

75   85   95

Age of Borrower

*With monthly compounding.

in the home, which can be realized on a sale, though reduced by selling expenses. This is illustrated in the diagram on the previous page.

If, however, the home does *not* increase in value, there will be little or no equity after 10 years. This is because the mortgage, with interest building up on it, will be almost the same as the home value in 10 years. And, if the home should decline in value, even slightly, it will be worth less than the mortgage within 10 years.

Fortunately, as long as the borrower lives in the home, there can be no required payments and no forced sale by the mortgage lender.

Notice in the example that at 5% annual growth in the value of the home, if the owner remains in the program beyond age 95, the mortgage amount becomes greater than the value of the home. In this case, the insurance company would suffer a loss, not the homeowner or her estate.

A reverse mortgage has many attractive features. All the income received is essentially tax-free. No payments are made against the mortgage and the title to the home remains with the homeowner.

There are a couple of cautions, however. For one, it's probably not wise to take a reverse mortgage at too early an age. One reason is that the younger you are, the longer you will be expected to live, with the result that the annuity payments will be lower than you may wish or need. Another reason is that the longer your life expectancy, the more unpaid interest will accumulate on your mortgage and the size of the mortgage available to you will be reduced.

The second caution is that you may not be entirely comfortable with the fact that you are carrying a significant debt at an older age. Many of us work hard to be relieved of debt and a reverse mortgage puts us back in that position. As well, depending on the importance of leaving a substantial estate, a reverse mortgage may not be best for you since the mortgage and accumulated interest will be paid to the mortgage company and not to your heirs or estate.

But if you are comfortable with the debt while you're living and feel that the equity built up in your home over the years should be yours to enjoy, a reverse mortgage may be an ideal means of increasing your income level to one that will allow you to enjoy your retirement years more fully.

CHAPTER 6

ESTATE PLANNING

E state planning is a subject that many people still aren't very comfortable discussing or even thinking about. It's a topic easy to ignore and put off until another day. Most people just don't seem to be able to "get around to it." Unfortunately, that's still the situation for about **half** of the population. Even among those who have a will and therefore feel (incorrectly) that they've got things taken care of, a large proportion haven't reviewed and updated their will within the last three years to bring it into alignment with new legislation or changed family circumstances.

There's also a widespread misconception that estate planning is only for the wealthy or for the elderly. In fact, if you have **any** assets to pass on, estate planning is necessary. It has almost nothing to do with wealth or age—it's something nearly everyone has a stake in.

Estate planning represents one of the best opportunities you will ever have to provide special gifts or benefits to those you love, not only after your death, but during your lifetime as well. You can make decisions that may have a huge positive impact on the lives of others. But without a plan, you can impose havoc, conflict, and hardship on people you love. *You can't take it with you, but you can determine how it will be left behind.*

• COACH'S PLAYBOOK •

In the estate planning process you want to ACHIEVE:

- ✓ maximized estate proceeds for your heirs
- ✓ distribution of assets in accordance with your wishes
- ✓ adequate provision for loved ones in the event of your death
- ✓ adequate liquidity in estate to pay any taxes and liabilities
- ✓ ensured guardianship for minor children
- ✓ the naming of a trusted personal or corporate executor to administer your estate

And you want to AVOID:

- ✓ needless taxation
- ✓ family strife
- ✓ delays in settling the estate
- ✓ costly legal challenges
- ✓ probate fees charged by the state
- ✓ loss of control of family assets such as vacation home, farm, or family business

By taking the following actions, you'll be able to achieve your estate planning goals.

PREPARE A VALID, UP-TO-DATE WILL

This is the foundation of any estate plan and it includes many aspects.

WHAT IS A WILL?

● A will is a legal document, signed in accordance with specific rules, that's designed to be the final statement of your wishes. Properly designed and worded, your will can ensure that your wishes are carried out with a minimum of expense or delay.

● It should be reviewed every three years or so to ensure it has not been affected by changes in legislation or family circumstances.

● It is implemented only on your death and remains private until that time.

● You may change or revoke the terms of your will at any time until your death as long as you are mentally competent to do so.

WHY IS A WILL IMPORTANT?

If you die without a will, a number of negative things can happen, including these:

● The beneficiaries of your estate will be determined by state law.

This is a huge consideration! I constantly meet mature, successful adults with a spouse, children, a home, a vacation home, and assets of substantial value who haven't been able to find the time to have a will drawn up. If they truly understood the consequences of dying without a will, they'd make a beeline to have one drawn up.

● The court will appoint an administrator for your estate and that person may not be the person you would have chosen. While it's often a spouse or family member who is chosen, it's still possible that you wouldn't have chosen that person. The court's choice can also lead to family strife and possible extra legal costs if a challenge is undertaken.

● Without a will, distribution to heirs can be delayed for a significant period of time since no one can act until an administrator has been appointed by the court. This too can cause strife and added legal expenses.

● The court may appoint a guardian for minor children, and the guardian may not be your choice. Surely, you know the perfect guardian for minor children is probably a relative or family friend. Can you be certain the court would choose that same person? Clearly not.

● The estate may be subject to needless taxation if it has not been properly arranged. Huge bites can be taken by both federal and state governments, whereas with a plan in place thousands of dollars in tax can be deferred or avoided.

• COACH'S PLAYBOOK •

If you die without a will (intestate), your estate is distributed according to state law. This is what you can expect in most states if you predecease:

A Spouse and No Children or Grandchildren:
Everything goes to your spouse.

A Spouse and One or More Children:
Either one-third or one-half of the estate goes to your spouse. The balance is divided equally among the children. If a child is a minor, a court-appointed guardian will administer the funds. (Surely you'd rather select the person to administer those funds, wouldn't you?)

A Spouse and Parent (No Brother or Sister):
In some states, everything goes to your spouse; in others, the spouse shares with the parent(s).

A Spouse and Brother(s) or Sister(s):
In some states, the spouse gets it all; in others he or she shares with surviving siblings.

Spouse, Parent(s), and Brother(s) or Sister(s):
All to spouse in some states; in others, the spouse shares with parents and siblings.

Brother(s) and Sister(s):

Surviving siblings share the estate equally; the child(ren) of a deceased brother or sister may "step into the shoes" of the brother or sister and receive his or her share.

No Spouse or Children:

The entire estate goes to the "next of kin" (closest relative), usually in this order:

1. Parent(s).

2. If neither parent survives, brother(s)/sister(s) (children of deceased siblings may share their parent's share).

3. If none survive, nephews/nieces.

4. If none survive, next of kin.

5. If no traceable kin, the entire estate escheats, or reverts to the state government. (Do you want that to happen?)

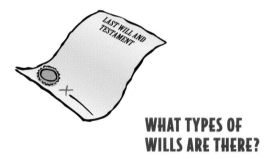

WHAT TYPES OF WILLS ARE THERE?

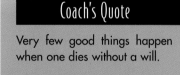

Coach's Quote

Very few good things happen when one dies without a will.

A *holographic* will is written in your handwriting and signed by you; no witness is necessary. A holographic will is **NOT** recommended since your words may not clearly express your interests and lead to controversy as to your actual wishes.

A *formal* will is typed and signed by you in front of at least two witnesses (who may not be one of your beneficiaries or their spouse). It is usually drafted by a lawyer so as to ensure clear and precise intent.

EXECUTOR SELECTION CHECKLIST

Here's a list of items to be considered when choosing your executor:

	YES	NO
1. Can this person act fairly and impartially toward all beneficiaries?	O	O
2. Is this person geographically accessible?	O	O
3. Can this person take time from his or her own job to devote to this task?	O	O
4. Could this person work well with the co-executors you may appoint?	O	O
5. Is this person likely to outlive you?	O	O
6. Is this person aware of the personal liability he or she assumes in case of errors he or she may make in carrying out the task?	O	O
7. Is this person knowledgeable in the areas of:		
• Estate and trust laws?	O	O
• Taxation of estates and trusts?	O	O
• Insurance?	O	O
• Real estate?	O	O
• Investments?	O	O
8. If not knowledgeable in these areas, is this person prepared to invest the time to become knowledgeable or to find experts to assist?	O	O
9. Does this person have and can he or she maintain a good personal relationship with the family?	O	O
10. Is this person prepared for and can he or she handle the potential criticism and challenges that may come from the family?	O	O
11. Has this person agreed to act as executor?	O	O

If the answers to these questions are predominantly "NO," you may want to look at other options or to involve a professional to assist your appointee.

Money Coach Rule

The will truly is the foundation of any estate plan, and there is very little excuse for a mature individual, especially one who cares about his or her family, not to have one in place. The modest cost of $300 to $500 is more than offset by the peace of mind that it offers, and the knowledge that you have provided a structure that your executor can use to ensure that your loved ones are cared for as you would want them to be.

HAVING A DURABLE POWER OF ATTORNEY AND A LIVING WILL

Many people who think they have a durable power of attorney and/or a Living Will do not, in fact. These terms are frequently misunderstood.

An ordinary power of attorney expires when the principal (you) becomes mentally incompetent, which is when you really need someone to act for you. A durable power of attorney serves this purpose.

A typical will is *testamentary;* that is, it becomes effective upon death. But there are often important medical decisions that must be made by others while the testator is still alive. A Living Will helps them make these decisions by stipulating your wishes concerning artificial, or "heroic," methods of prolonging your life.

So let's have a closer look at this important item.

Coach's Quote

In a word, the power of attorney is probably one of the most important documents you will ever sign, and everyone 18 or over should have one.

WHAT IS A POWER OF ATTORNEY FOR FINANCIAL AFFAIRS?

It's a document given in writing by the principal (you) to another person (the agent, who is called the attorney—not to be confused with "lawyer") to act on your behalf in conducting your financial affairs. It does not extend to decisions regarding medical treatment (see page 117). When you give someone this power of attorney, they can immediately sign documents on your behalf if you can't, either because you are away and unavailable or because you are ill. Because of the broad range of the power given, it's obviously important to select this person wisely. Note that all powers of attorney terminate in the event that the person you appoint dies, or in the event of your death. You can revoke a power of attorney at any time if you are mentally competent.

A normal power of attorney is a legal document that gives one or more people the authority to manage your financial affairs. It can be "general," covering all aspects of your financial affairs, or it can be "limited" to specific aspects. It would be valid only as long as you were mentally competent.

A durable power of attorney will continue to be valid **even in the event of your incapacitation,** which is probably the condition under which it would be most useful. Creation of a durable power can ensure that ongoing decisions can be made that are in your best interests. For this reason a spouse is normally given such authority.

A durable power of attorney comes in one of two forms. One is the "spring" or "springing" power of attorney. This "springs" into effect "when I [that's you, the principal] become incapacitated." The second type is valid "notwithstanding my capacity," that is, whether you are competent or not.

It is important to give a power of attorney only to the most trustworthy person. You can revoke it while you are still competent; if you do, make sure to reclaim all originals. Otherwise, the former appointee can present to banks, brokers, and transfer agents a form that appears valid.

YOU NEED BOTH POWER OF ATTORNEY AND A WILL

It's important to have both a durable power of attorney and a will. You see, with a power of attorney, you give your agent the power to act while you are alive but unable to act for yourself. The power of attorney is terminated on your death. At this point, the will takes effect and the executor/executrix named in your will has authority to act.

Therefore, be aware that the person appointed as your executor has **no authority or power** to act for you while you are alive. Even if you are legally incapacitated, the executor cannot act. Only your agent, called attorney-in-fact, appointed through a durable power of attorney, has the power to act while you are alive but unable to act for yourself.

It's for these reasons that we need **both** a will and a durable power of attorney.

WHY IS A DURABLE POWER OF ATTORNEY USEFUL?

There are many useful applications of a durable power of attorney, including these:

● Not only can the person appointed act on your behalf as soon as the documents are signed, he or she would also be able to act for you **even if** you were to become incapacitated. The power you grant continues and "endures" beyond your incapacitation and is therefore referred to as a durable or enduring power of attorney.

● Remember that a **normal** power of attorney is valid only as long as you are mentally competent. The real advantage of the durable power of attorney is its enduring nature, which makes it useful at just the times (i.e., times of mental incompetency due to accident or disease), when a normal power of attorney becomes invalid.

● If you are a businessperson, the durable power of attorney enables you to appoint someone to look after your business affairs if you are unable to because of accident or sickness.

● In some states, in order to sell or refinance the family home, the law requires the signature of both spouses on the deed or mortgage even though it may be registered in one spouse's name alone. Therefore, if one spouse is incapacitated, without the durable power of attorney, the second spouse is handcuffed. With it, such sale or refinancing could be undertaken.

● It is an invaluable tool in protecting yourself and your family against the possibility of a court-appointed trustee taking **complete** management control of **all** your financial affairs.

Money Coach Rule

For many of the same reasons outlined earlier regarding a durable power of attorney for property, it's important that you have a Living Will and a power of attorney for health care in place as soon as possible. By taking such actions now, you'll significantly increase the likelihood of your being able to die with dignity.

HAVE A HEALTH CARE DURABLE POWER OF ATTORNEY

A health care durable power of attorney allows you to appoint an agent to make health care decisions should you become unable to do so yourself. Ordinarily, the power of attorney given is limited to personal care, including medical decisions. The agent has no authority in financial or business decisions.

A Living Will is typically a "treatment directive." It is prepared when one is competent to make a decision as to the future use of life support for medical purposes. It stipulates that no extraordinary life-sustaining medical procedures be used to prolong life when there is no hope of recovery. Although it may not be legally enforceable, this document serves as evidence to physicians, courts, and relatives of the patient's wishes as recorded when he or she was in a competent state of mind.

Forms for preparing Living Wills may be obtained from Choice in Dying (New York City) and other similar organizations or hospitals.

AVOID UNNECESSARY PROBATE FEES

What Is Probate?

Probate is a legal process that confirms a will. Usually the executor and/or your lawyer files for probate with the appropriate court. The names of courts vary. In New York State, it is Surrogate's Court. In California, it is Superior Court. In Pennsylvania, it is Orphan's Court. Elsewhere it may be Probate, County, or Circuit Court.

Once the will has been processed, the court issues testamentary letters, which confirm the authority of the person acting under the will. Financial institutions will not normally release the assets of an estate to an executor until they receive proof of testamentary letters.

MINIMIZE ESTATE TAXES

A steep federal estate tax is imposed on estates that exceed a market value of $600,000[1] at the time of death or on the alternate valuation date, which is six months after death. To use the alternate valuation date, the estate's market value and tax must be less than they were as of the date of death.

The federal estate tax is essentially collected on the transfer to the next generation. For example, there is an unlimited marital deduction. If one leaves one's estate entirely to one's spouse, there is no tax on the estate, no matter how large it is. When the spouse dies, however, in the absence of remarriage, there will be no spouse to leave it to, so the entire estate from the original couple will be taxed, minus the $600,000[1] exemption.

Using a unified credit trust, it is possible for a couple to enjoy two $600,000[1] exemptions. A brief explanation of what a trust is and how it works is provided later in this chapter.

---

[1] The $600,000 exemption will be increased in steps after 1998. See Table 6-2 on page 122.

Federal Estate Tax Rate

The federal estate tax allows an estate tax credit of $192,800 for 1997. The way it works is that $192,800 is exactly the tax on an estate worth $600,000 at death. In other words, the first $600,000[1] of net assets that a person leaves passes to heirs free of federal estate taxes because the credit equals the tax. For estates valued at more than $600,000[1], estate tax rates are graduated from 37% to 55% (see Table 6-1 below). In addition, there may be a state estate tax (also based on the value of the estate) or a state inheritance tax based on the amount that an heir receives. State taxes vary widely among the 50 states.

Table 6-1—Unified Rate Schedule

Column A	Column B	Column C	Column D
Taxable amount over	Taxable amount not over	Tax on amount in column A	Rate of tax on excess over amount in column A
			Percent
$ 0	$ 10,000	$ 0	18
10,000	20,000	1,800	20
20,000	40,000	3,800	22
40,000	60,000	8,200	24
60,000	80,000	13,000	26
80,000	100,000	18,200	28
100,000	150,000	23,800	30
150,000	250,000	38,800	32
250,000	500,000	70,800	34
500,000	750,000	155,800	37
750,000	1,000,000	248,300	39
1,000,000	1,250,000	345,800	41
1,250,000	1,500,000	448,300	43
1,500,000	2,000,000	555,800	45
2,000,000	2,500,000	780,800	49
2,500,000	3,000,000	1,025,800	53
3,000,000	. . . .	1,290,800	55

Note: The most relevant portion of the table is where column A exceeds $600,000.

State Tax Credit

The federal estate tax allows a uniform credit for state death taxes paid to the individual state. This means that death taxes paid to a state reduce federal estate taxes dollar for dollar, up to the limit of the uniform state death tax credit allowed. However, those who died in a state with a high estate tax get no extra deduction for their federal estate tax.

Suppose that Mrs. Rose died in 1997, leaving a taxable estate of $1,250,000. This represents the market value of all of her assets less liabilities at death, reduced by expenses of her estate such as legal and accounting fees, executor fees, and funeral and burial expenses.

The estate tax on the $1,250,000 she left is $448,300 (see Table 6-1). From that amount the unified credit is subtracted (everyone gets $192,800 unless this was used up through excessive lifetime gifts) and the State Death Tax Credit is subtracted to derive the federal estate tax payable. The maximum state death tax credit is found in Table 6-3. The Adjusted Taxable Estate is the taxable estate minus $60,000. In this case the adjusted taxable estate is $1,190,000, which allows a state death credit of $48,400. Provided that the estate paid the individual state that amount or more, a credit may be claimed of up to $48,400 against the federal tax.

Our federal estate tax payable is $207,100 as shown below:

Tax	$448,400
Less: Unified credit	192,800
Less: State Death Tax credit	48,400
Amount of estate tax due	$207,100

Reducing Estate Taxes

There are numerous ways to reduce estate taxes, and they should be considered with the advice of experts such as a CPA, attorney, or financial planner. The purpose of proper planning is to achieve some non-tax goal concerning the orderly transfer of assets in the manner desired, to whom desired, and also to reduce taxes.

Trusts. Trusts, defined later in this chapter, are a common way to accomplish both non-tax and tax goals. The unified credit trust is one of the most popular and effective ways to reduce estate taxes for married couples with more than $600,000[1] of net assets. A typical one works like this: According to the will, which was prepared with this as a foremost consideration, upon the death of the first spouse, up to $600,000[1] worth of assets is placed in a "unified credit" trust. Income such as dividends and interest from these assets may be paid to the surviving spouse quarterly. This assures the surviving spouse of money to live on. Upon the spouse's eventual death, the trust principal, which may still be worth $600,000[1], more or less, passes to the children without a federal estate tax. In addition, a second $600,000[1] exemption is applied to assets held outside the trust by the second spouse to die. By using a unified credit trust, each person at death utilizes the $600,000[1] exemption, allowing $1.2 million[1] to be transferred without federal estate tax. In the absence of such a program, as designed and drafted in the will, only one amount of $600,000[1] would be exempt.

Asset Values. As a general rule, all assets are included in an estate at their fair market value at the time of death (or the alternate valuation date). There are important exceptions for valuation of a closely held business or farm if certain conditions are met; such exceptions allow such possible benefits as an extended period of time to pay estate taxes, with interest at a low rate. Another provision is to value a farm according to its current use rather than the much greater value of its highest and best use. These tax-saving opportunities may bring certain burdens, however, such as a requirement that the family continue farming operations for many years.

Life Insurance. Have a relative own the policy on your life. Upon your death the value of the policy may not be included in your taxable estate.

Family Limited Partnership. Another method of reducing estate asset values is to form a family limited partnership and place major assets in it. As compared to outright sole ownership of a property, the value of a limited partnership interest may be much less. Of course, this mechanism may bring such cumbersome and awkward non-tax consequences as attempts to sell a limited partnership interest.

Capable assistance may be needed to help transfer a business or assets to the next generation.

Gifts. Gifts may be used to greatly reduce one's estate. Every year one may give up to $10,000 to another person without affecting the estate tax exemption. Married couples may join together in their gifts. Accordingly, Grandma and Grandpa together can give you $20,000 a year, plus another $20,000 to your spouse and the same to each of your three children. That way, their estate is reduced by $100,000 per year through gifts to you and your family. If your brother or sister also has a family of five, another $100,000 can be given each year. Should more than $10,000 per person per year be given, the excess reduces the $600,000 estate tax exemption (that may soon be increased by Congress) at death. The $10,000 gift amount is potentially indexed for inflation. However, inflation adjustments become effective when inflation raises the $10,000 by $1,000 increments.

Property Received

Many people don't realize that gifts received are not taxable income to the recipient. Similarly, a sum received from an inheritance is not taxable income.

Stepped-up Basis. Heirs inherit property at a "stepped-up tax basis" at death. That is, the unrealized appreciation of an asset escapes taxation upon one's death. This is one of the great tax loopholes of all time.

Example 1: Your mother died and left you $100,000 worth of stock in a publicly held company, for which she paid $2,000. The $98,000 of unrealized gain is never subject to income taxation. You (the heir) receive the stock with a tax basis of $100,000, the value at death. If you sell it for $100,000, there is no gain or loss.

Example 2: Your father died, leaving you an apartment building worth $500,000. During the 25 years that he owned the building, he depreciated it for income tax purposes to the point of having an adjusted tax basis approaching zero. You inherit it at a tax basis of $500,000 and can start depreciating it there.

Thus, for the heir's tax purposes, the tax basis is "stepped up" to the date of death. None of the appreciation that accumulated before death is taxed for income tax purposes.

Table 6-2—Estate Exclusion Amounts	
In the Case of Estates of Decendents Dying, and Gifts Made During:	The Applicable Exclusion Amount Is:
1998	$625,000
1999	$650,000
2000 and 2001	$675,000
2002 and 2003	$700,000
2004	$850,000
2005	$950,000
2006 or thereafter	$1,000,000

STATE SUCCESSION TAXES

Nearly every state imposes an estate tax, inheritance tax, or both. While each state has its own laws and rates, many states have adopted the same tax schedule as the federal credit for state death taxes, which is shown in Table 6-3.

Table 6-3—Credit for State Death Taxes

Adjusted Taxable Estate					Of Excess
At least	But less than	Credit =	+	%	Over
$ 0	$ 40,000	$ 0	0	$ 0
40,000	90,000	0	0.8	40,000
90,000	140,000	400	1.6	90,000
140,000	240,000	1,200	2.4	140,000
240,000	440,000	3,600	3.2	240,000
440,000	640,000	10,000	4.0	440,000
640,000	840,000	18,000	4.8	640,000
840,000	1,040,000	27,600	5.6	840,000
1,040,000	1,540,000	38,800	6.4	1,040,000
1,540,000	2,040,000	70,800	7.2	1,540,000
2,040,000	2,540,000	106,800	8.0	2,040,000
2,540,000	3,040,000	146,800	8.8	2,540,000
3,040,000	3,540,000	190,800	9.6	3,040,000
3,540,000	4,040,000	238,800	10.4	3,540,000
4,040,000	5,040,000	290,800	11.2	4,040,000
5,040,000	6,040,000	402,800	12.0	5,040,000
6,040,000	7,040,000	522,800	12.8	6,040,000
7,040,000	8,040,000	650,800	13.6	7,040,000
8,040,000	9,040,000	786,800	14.4	8,040,000
9,040,000	10,040,000	930,800	15.2	9,040,000
10,040,000	. . . .	1,082,800	16.0	10,040,000

Table 6-4—Probate Timeline

The following outline traces the time sequence of a typical probate. However, because state probate laws vary, this table cannot account for any particular estate.

Task	When Performed
File petition for probate of will or for testamentary letters of administration in intestacy	Within 30 days after death
Publish or post notice to creditors	Immediately upon granting of petition for probate
Apply for family or widow's allowance or probate homestead	Immediately upon granting of petition for probate
Gather assets and prepare formal inventory of estate; present to appraiser if required	Promptly after executor assumes his office

Task	When Performed
Period for notice to creditors elapses	Varies widely; normally 2–6 months after first publication or posting
Sell estate property to raise cash for taxes or distribution	Any time after executor is appointed
Make preliminary distributions	Usually after notice-to-creditors period elapses
Prepare and file state inheritance tax papers	Usually 6–9 months after appointment of executor
Alternate valuation date for federal estate tax purposes	6 months after date of death
Where no federal estate tax return required, make final accounting and distribution, and close estate	Approximately one month after notice-to-creditors period elapses and state taxes paid
File federal estate tax return (Form 706) and pay federal estate taxes	9 months after date of death, unless extensions applied for and granted
If no wish to wait for audit of federal return, make final accounting and distribution, and close estate	Approximately 1–2 months after estate tax paid
Keep estate open until federal return is audited or audit period elapses	3 years after estate tax return is filed
When audit period elapses, make final accounting and distribution, and close estate	1–3 months after audit period elapses
To keep income tax advantages of probate estate, keep estate open	As long as possible

HOW CAN PROBATE FEES BE REDUCED?

These suggestions should be considered only with professional advice:

- Make your spouse your IRA beneficiary. This will make it possible for the funds in your plan(s) to pass directly to your spouse without tax and without becoming part of your estate and therefore without incurring probate costs. Assets passing to a spouse upon death are not subject to federal estate tax because the marital deduction is unlimited.

- Name an adult person, rather than your estate, as beneficiary of your life insurance policies and annuity contracts. This strategy may preclude these assets from becoming part of your estate and therefore avoid probate costs.

● Hold other assets as joint tenants. These assets include your home, real estate investments, bank accounts, mutual funds, stocks, bonds, and other assets. Jointly held assets pass automatically to the surviving owner if one dies, without going into the estate and therefore without probate fees being charged.

● Convert personal debt to corporate debt. Most personal debt is not a deduction for the purpose of determining a person's probatable estate. Therefore, it may be wise to move assets that have debt attached to them to a corporation, so that a deduction can effectively be taken on the debt. The asset that would fall into the estate for probate purposes would then be the shares of the company, not the investment portfolio. In valuing the company shares, all debts of the corporation would be included.

● Create a private holding company in a low-probate state.

● Set up a living (or "inter vivos") trust. Assets held in a trust do not pass to your estate after death. A trust can be an effective estate planning device that is very flexible and can, for example, allow you to access its capital or income during your life. On death, assets pass to your intended beneficiaries according to the trust document—not the will. **The result: no probate fees**.

A NOTE OF CAUTION

These options are intended to reduce probate fees, but the area of estate planning is quite complex. Some of the techniques described may impact other aspects of the process, including other potential tax liabilities and family law. To be sure, discuss the overall plan with your financial advisor, who may wish to take legal or accounting counsel as well.

CONSIDER LIFE INSURANCE

While we usually consider the primary purpose of life insurance as replacing the income of the insured in case of death, it can have other importance as part of a well-developed estate plan.

In this context, appropriate levels of life insurance can provide liquidity within an estate to pay off liabilities such as taxes, probate fees, or mortgages

AN EXAMPLE:

Perhaps the best example of how life insurance can be used as an estate planning tool is a situation like this:

On your father's death, all his assets were passed on to your mother as part of the unlimited marital deduction, and no federal estate taxes were payable at that time.

Now, however, your mother has passed away and, on the day of her death, all her capital assets are included in her estate at fair market value. Note that the assets were not sold; they are valued *as if they had been sold* at fair market value. If the value of an estate at death is more than $600,000[1], there is a federal estate tax, payable at rates of 37% to 55%, on the excess over $600,000[1].

One major asset held by your mother, a large and valuable piece of land, had been in the family for years and had grown substantially in value. When this property was valued at its fair market value (as if it had been sold), the federal estate tax owed by your mother's estate was $100,000.

Without insurance coverage, it's quite possible that, lacking other assets in her estate that could be sold to pay the tax, the land itself would have to be sold. If the real estate market was soft at the time of her death, it's quite possible that the sale might not bring much money—possibly not even enough to cover the tax liability.

Fortunately, your mother had good advice from her financial advisor, had calculated the taxes due on her death, and had purchased $100,000 of term life insurance to cover the liability. There is therefore no need to sell any of the estate's assets and thus diminish its size. Thanks to her prudent planning, the beneficiaries of the estate will be in a much-improved position. The only two drawbacks to this strategy are that the person seeking to use life insurance as an estate planning tool may not be insurable and the cost of term life insurance for the elderly is quite high.

and thus protect more of the estate's assets for its beneficiaries. It can also be used to ensure that in settling the estate, less liquid assets such as real estate might not need to be sold under duress and at a less-than-attractive price.

CONSIDER THE USE OF TRUSTS

WHAT IS A TRUST?

The concept of a trust goes back to about the Middle Ages. They were first used widely during the period of the Crusades, when individuals were away from home for prolonged periods. At such a time, it was important to create the means by which business and personal decisions could be carried out on one's behalf by someone else.

Money Coach Rule

And as a final twist on the idea, how about this?

What about discussing this strategy with your children, who may be beneficiaries of your estate, and suggest that they consider paying your annual insurance premium? You have created the means by which part of their inheritance can be protected from the tax man, and yet you incur no extra costs in doing so if your beneficiaries pay the annual premium.

Simply stated, a trust involves the holding of trust property by one person for the benefit of another.

To create a valid trust, there must be a trustor (also called the settlor), a trustee, and identifiable beneficiaries. Not all three parties must be different; for example, one person could be the settlor and also be a trustee. This could happen if parents were to create a trust during their lifetime for a child who was a dependent. A trustor could also be one of several trustees; but it is not legal to have a situation where the trustor is also the trustee and the sole beneficiary.

A trust can come into existence when legal title to some property has been transferred to a trustee, and, although the trustee has legal title

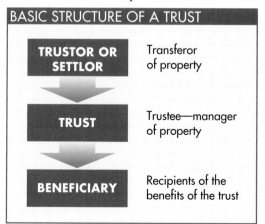

BASIC STRUCTURE OF A TRUST

TRUSTOR OR SETTLOR	Transferor of property
TRUST	Trustee—manager of property
BENEFICIARY	Recipients of the benefits of the trust

to the trust property, beneficial ownership rests with the beneficiaries.

Many types of assets can be put into a trust, including bank accounts, shares of private businesses, stocks, bonds, mutual funds, and real estate.

TYPES OF TRUSTS

There are many different types and uses of trusts, but we're going to introduce only the main types; we're not dealing here with "corporate trusts" or "offshore trusts" because they can become very complex and have convoluted tax and legal implications.

The two main types of trusts are **"living trusts"** and **"testamentary trusts."**

Living Trusts (Sometimes Called Inter Vivos or Family Trusts)

A living trust, not surprisingly, is created while an individual is alive and comes into operation once the trust agreement is signed and the trust is funded.

A living trust may continue to exist after the trustor dies, or there may be provisions within the trust agreement whereby the trustee is given directions to terminate or collapse the trust and distribute the assets to the beneficiaries on the trustor's death.

A classic use to which a living trust is put is to transfer beneficial ownership of an asset to an intended beneficiary while still maintaining control over the asset. It would allow you, for example, to provide income from a trust to a spouse or child, while retaining control of the capital. It may apply where shares of a family business are placed in trust and yet the trustor wishes to continue to have influence in the business.

Living trusts can be designed as either **"revocable"** or **"irrevocable."** Revocable living trusts allow the trustor to change his/her mind and reclaim some or all of the assets within the trust. However, the Internal Revenue Code severely curtails the tax advantages of revocable living trusts, and, since the tax advantages are usually important considerations in establishing the trust in the first place, most living trusts are irrevocable. It's the permanent legal change in ownership that creates the tax advantages and estate planning opportunities of living trusts.

Testamentary Trusts

A testamentary trust takes effect upon your death, and the items establishing and providing for its operation are included in your will. Testamentary trusts, such as a unified credit trust, are funded out of the proceeds of the deceased's estate. Before one's death, one can modify the terms of the trust or even remove it, simply by having a new will created. Because it's not technically established until one's death, its terms can be kept as private as one's will. And of course, by their nature, testamentary trusts are irrevocable.

Discretionary/Nondiscretionary

Both living and testamentary trusts can be established as **"discretionary"** or **"nondiscretionary."** A discretionary trust allows the trustee to use guidelines or to use discretion in determining the income to be paid to a beneficiary. For example, the trustee(s) may decide to use capital of the trust to allow a student beneficiary to pay tuition and expenses for university, medical school, or graduate school, even though it may erode the original capital of the trust. If, in the trustees' mind, the primary intent of the trust was to fund such expenses rather than to retain the full original capital, they may use their discretion to make such payments before the date of intended distribution. A nondiscretionary trust does not contain documentary provision for trustee(s) to use discretion prior to the date of intended distribution.

Testamentary trusts can also be used to allow the testator to identify the purpose for which funds can be spent and may include educational costs, the purchase of a first home, or nearly any other identified purpose. This approach is effective when the testator is unsure of how the funds might be spent if given without stated intent to a beneficiary not mature enough to make decisions on his or her own behalf.

Trusts are often useful to people in a second marriage who have children from a previous marriage. A trust can be set up so that the second spouse receives income for life from the trust assets. Following the second spouse's death, the remaining trust assets can be diverted to the children from the first marriage. Without a trust, assets could pass to the second spouse's beneficiaries.

• COACH'S PLAYBOOK •

Differences between living and testamentary trusts

Item	Living	Testamentary
Creation	Created during person's lifetime and begins to operate when funded.	Created by will and begins to operate on death of individual.
Assets Into Trust	Assets transferred from trustor's (settlor's) name to trustee's name.	Assets flow to trust from deceased's estate.
Trustee(s)	Anyone including trustor (settlor).	Anyone (obviously excluding trustor, now deceased), and often the deceased's executor.
Discretionary/ Nondiscretionary	May be either.	May be either.

TRUSTS AND TAXES

As trusts have evolved from their origins during the Medieval period, they have come to be associated with tax planning to a greater and greater degree. There are certain critical tax advantages in certain trusts. This is by no means to suggest that they have only tax advantages, but rather that they should be considered for **tax reasons AND for estate planning reasons**.

PREPLAN FUNERAL ARRANGEMENTS

A prearranged funeral is a funeral arrangement made before death. It's a practical way of identifying your wishes for your own funeral, or for the funeral of someone for whom you are responsible.

WHAT ARE THE ADVANTAGES?

A prearranged funeral is part of a sensible estate plan. When you discuss a prearranged funeral with a funeral director, you have an opportunity to ask questions and to be sure you fully understand what services are provided and at what cost. You can make unhurried decisions regarding the type of service you wish, the type of casket you desire, and your preferences for burial, entombment, or cremation. Such planning will serve as a helpful guide for family and friends and just seems to make practical sense.

WHY PREARRANGE A FUNERAL?

Planning for a funeral now will save others that responsibility later. Providing guidelines can only make things easier at a time of emotion and stress.

A number of nursing homes now require that funeral arrangements be in place before a resident enters a home. Also, health care professionals often recommend that families caring for terminally ill individuals make funeral arrangements.

It's also important to remember that while the funeral is for the person who has died, it also allows the survivors to satisfy their own emotional and psychological needs. For this reason, preplanning can allow room for the wishes of the family as to how the funeral should be conducted. So discussion with family, friends, clergy, and executor is an important part of funeral prearrangement.

PREPLANNING MAKES SENSE

FOR YOU	FOR THE FAMILY
You select what you desire.	They know it's what you wanted.
You decide in the comfort of your home.	They'll have more time for family and friends.
You aren't rushed.	They won't need to make any hasty decisions.
You can save money.	They won't be financially burdened.
You enjoy peace of mind.	They will thank you.

ESTATE PLANNING CHECKLIST

(Check your estate planning progress as you accomplish each step.)

ITEM	DONE
1. I have prepared a valid up-to-date will.	○
2. I have a durable power of attorney.	○
3. I have a power of attorney for health care.	○
4. I have prepared a Living Will.	○
5. I have assured that my estate will not be subjected to unnecessary probate fees.	○
6. I have a record of personal affairs.	○
7. I have registered property jointly (where appropriate).	○
8. I have reviewed the consideration of life insurance.	○
9. I have reviewed the consideration of trusts.	○
10. I have assured that my estate will not be subjected to any unnecessary tax.	○
11. I have given gifts to family members (where possible).	○
12. I have preplanned all funeral arrangements.	○
13. I have given to charity on a preplanned basis.	○

CHAPTER 7

I f you wish to build financial freedom for yourself and your family, it's
essential to begin the task as soon as possible. The principles I've outlined
so far will put you on the right track. If you stick with them over the long
term, you are virtually assured of outstanding success.

The sooner you apply them, the sooner and more effectively you'll be
ensuring financial independence not only for yourself but also for future
generations of your family!

Here's an example of how time and consistency along with the "magic" of
compounding can ensure financial freedom for generations to come:

Let's assume you start with nothing—which is probably as true for you as
it was for me.

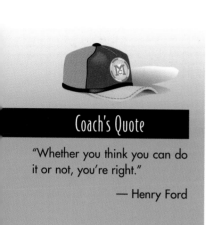

You begin by saving $100 per month—more would be better, of course. In 20 years at a compound rate of 12%, you would have $98,926.

Now, let's say you wish to send your two children to college for a total of eight years, so you stop depositing $100 a month. Instead, you withdraw $10,000 per year ($5,000 every six months) for a total withdrawal of $80,000. Your original $98,926 minus the $80,000 would actually have grown to $127,154 (let's hear it for compounding!).

Now let's go even further and assume that you resume deposits of $100 per month for 30 more years. Your $98,926 would grow to over $3.7 million!

Your children and their children of course continue to save $100 a month, and for generations your family will be able to use the investment that you started for education, housing, travel, emergencies, and so forth, and still pass it on to the next generations.

But as always, it's important to start now. As a friend of mine commented, "I should have started doing this stuff 20 years ago." I agreed. The best time to start was 20 years ago. The second-best time to start is now!

Don't be discouraged by lost opportunities; focus on creating new opportunities for yourself, for your children, and for your children's children.

Your altitude is determined by your attitude—attitude is everything!

There are books full of excuses for not acting: "The timing's not quite right." "I don't have any money." "I'm too busy right now." "I could never force myself to do that!"

All the education and knowledge available about how to become financially independent means absolutely nothing if you don't use that knowledge by applying it. It takes only a decision, a commitment, and a few dollars to start you on your way. Remember, it doesn't take a fortune to make a fortune; all it takes is some time.

But, the sad truth is that most people will not act because they simply don't believe it can work for them. They've conditioned themselves to accept being average and ordinary, to accept financial difficulty, to accept being poor, and to accept being unhappy.

Fortunately, as I lecture in different cities, I'm seeing growing numbers of people who view themselves differently—they see themselves as winners. They think and act like winners, and they become winners. They're the people who can stay motivated and stick to their plan to achieve financial independence for as long as it takes to happen.

"THE TIMING'S NOT QUITE RIGHT"

I'm noticing too that these often tend to be people who have their version of a money coach to work with, who helps them stay on course. Most definitely, there is a price to pay and priorities to be established and stuck to.

"I DON'T REALLY NEED SECURITY"

But I don't know anybody who has achieved financial independence who doesn't look back and say: "Yes, there was a price to pay, but, believe me, it was worth it!" Several of these people have told me too that if they had known how fantastic it would feel to be financially independent, they would have been willing to pay a much bigger price than they actually did.

Remember, a winning, healthy, positive attitude is not with us at birth. It is not the result of an injection or a pill, it is not part of a university degree program, and it is definitely not for sale. It's much simpler than that! (I've said all along that the great truths are the simplest!) It's the result of a simple decision that you have the ability to make. A decision to be extraordinary rather than ordinary, happy rather than sad, positive rather than negative, wealthy rather than poor—in short, a decision to be a winner in all areas of life.

"I'M TOO BUSY RIGHT NOW"

Remember the goal? It's to create a situation whereby you retire at the same level of income as you enjoyed during your peak earning years. It's going to happen because you make it happen through a simple but deliberate long-term plan. It's going to happen over a period of time because you have not only learned what needs to be done—you have done what needs to be done.

INVESTMENT BEHAVIORS OF THE RICH

Over the last several years, considerable research has been conducted on the topic of the attitudes and behavior of affluent investors, both in Canada and the United States. In the United States, the Securities Industry Association has conducted annual research on the topic since the late 1980s. U.S. Trust conducted a survey of the most affluent 1% of Americans in late 1992.

In Canada, Decima Research conducted a poll on behalf of Royal Trust to examine the priorities and attitudes of the most affluent 25% of the population in the fall of 1994, and at the same time NCE Resources commissioned Dun & Bradstreet along with J. White and Associates to examine the most affluent 1% of Canadians.

Fascinating patterns about these individuals emerge from the data gathered on a broad range of issues, from their attitudes toward money, their view of the future, their concerns over rising taxes, the state of government pensions, their investment habits, and their attitude toward estate planning.

Below, we identify six specific behaviors that seem to distinguish the rich from the rest. This is done in the belief that we can often learn from others by simply watching and noting what they do—and then copying their behavior. As investors try to learn from the investing greats such as Sir John Templeton, Warren Buffett, Bob Krembil, and others, so can we learn to be financially successful from those who have already done so. Here's what they do:

1. THEY USE STRATEGIC ASSET ALLOCATION TO CREATE A WELL-BALANCED PORTFOLIO

These folks know that a Nobel Prize was awarded to Dr. William F. Sharpe of Stanford University and Dr. Harry M. Markowitz of the University of Chicago in 1990 for studies carried out over the previous several decades that led to breakthrough research confirming that we can **increase returns and reduce risk** through the use of Strategic Asset Allocation. This research proved academically what many know intuitively: it's best not to put all your eggs in one basket.

And so these investors diversified their portfolios both geographically and by asset class. They are much more likely for example to invest internationally than middle-class Americans. They are also much more likely to use a broad range of asset categories that include real estate, inflation hedges like gold and oil and gas, and both U.S. and international equities rather than limiting themselves, as others are more inclined to, to cash and fixed-income investments.

They use a balanced portfolio because they know from Sharpe and Markowitz's research (subsequently reinforced and validated by numerous other scientific studies) that 80% to 90% of a portfolio's return comes as a result of the mix or balance of assets within it; this asset allocation decision is the **single most important investment decision we make.** They have learned that such considerations as market timing and different management styles are of comparatively minor significance. They also know that the choice of individual security (be it stock, bond, or mutual fund) is among the least significant factor—despite the fact that this is the decision **most** people spend **most** time on. They therefore construct a balanced portfolio—and let it work for them.

2. THEY BELIEVE IN AND USE EQUITIES

Over and over again, research from all over the world demonstrates clearly that over the longer term, equities outperform other asset categories—specifically the fixed-income alternative on which Americans have historically been fixated.

The most affluent understand that equities represent the "engine" or the "locomotive" of an investment portfolio, and that equities are an absolutely necessary component to ensure results that will vault our returns ahead of taxes and inflation.

They understand too that equities are more favorably taxed than fixed-income vehicles.

And so we find that nearly 60% of America's rich have 31% or more of their portfolios in equities, as compared to the middle class, where only about 16% of investors have that much in equities.

Could it possibly be that an **understanding** of the value of equities, combined with actually **using** them in a portfolio, helps to make the rich rich? Absolutely!

3. THEY USE MUTUAL FUNDS

The rich know the value of hiring professionals to assist them in achieving their goals. The use of mutual funds for them is a logical extension of this understanding. They often don't have the time, the inclination, maybe even the expertise to identify the specific components of their investment portfolio. And so nearly 75% of the rich use mutual funds compared to between 30% and 40% of the rest of the population.

4. THEY USE TAX SHELTER OPPORTUNITIES

The best tax shelter available to Americans (next to their home) is the TRSP, and the rich take full advantage of the opportunity. Virtually all of them make the full contribution allowed!

It's true that beyond their TSRP, the rich, like the rest of Americans, do not make as much use of other tax shelter opportunities, including mutual fund limited partnerships, oil and gas funds, and others as they might. Much of this is attributed to the fact that they just don't **know** very much about these options yet. The rich do, however, seem to be more receptive to tax shelter opportunities than the population at large.

5. THEY HAVE AN ESTATE PLAN IN PLACE

Nearly 90% of the rich have an estate plan, including a current will, in place, as compared to only about 40% of the middle class.

They seem to understand the dangers of dying without a will ("intestate"), which include the fact that their assets may well be distributed by a public official in a way quite contrary to their wishes—and they've taken steps to prevent that from happening.

As part of their estate plan, they are also likely to have taken steps to reduce the amount of estate taxes and to have in place a durable power of attorney that will allow for a smooth administration of their assets in the event of their mental and/or physical incapacity.

An estate plan is necessary for **everyone** who has assets to pass along, regardless of the size of the assets or age.

It seems from these statistics that the rich are not only more determined to grow their assets; they are also more determined to preserve them.

6. THEY USE FINANCIAL ADVISORS

According to the NCE study, the rich are 3¹/₂ times more likely than the rest of the population to use the services of a financial advisor. Many of those interviewed stated categorically that the advice they received prompted them to do the very things that assisted them to become wealthy: to develop a balanced portfolio, to include equities in their portfolio, to use mutual funds, to use tax shelter opportunities, and to develop a comprehensive estate plan.

In fact, a groundbreaking study conducted in the United States from January 1983 to September 1993 asked the question: "Do the services of an independent financial planner make a difference?" The results were conclusive. U.S. mutual fund investors who purchased mutual funds through an independent advisor did nearly 20% better than those who purchased no-load funds on their own.

Similar results were found in a similar study conducted in Canada. Interviews were conducted with 1,890 Canadians to determine their financial performance over the three-year period between 1989 and 1992. Those who used the services of an independent financial advisor realized net asset growth that was 34% higher than the financial returns achieved by investors who made their own financial decisions and did not receive outside professional advice during that three-year time period.

Since this period was one of the most volatile in modern investment history, these results should not be surprising. The superior, professionally advised returns on invested capital was most often achieved by following advice to move assets out of real estate and fixed-income securities into bond funds, international equities, and domestic mutual funds as well as learning to anticipate the interest rate cycle.

Furthermore, 90% of the rich update their financial plan annually or more than once a year. They understand the Chinese proverb that, "If you don't know where you're going, any road will do." These people have a very clear idea of where they are going and they are receiving assistance to get there.

Only 10% of the rest of the population makes use of the services of a financial advisor, which may help to account for the fact that this huge majority of Americans are simply not, on a consistent basis, taking some of the relatively few but immensely important actions that can literally make them rich, at least in a financial sense.

CONCLUSION

It's not necessary to reinvent the wheel. We can learn by watching and imitating successful people in almost every walk of life, from sports to business, to entertainment to finance.

If the rich are more financially successful because they use a balanced portfolio approach with a significant position in equities, because they have retirement and estate plans, because they use the services of investment managers and financial advisors, and because they use key tax reduction opportunities, then perhaps, just perhaps, middle-income Americans could follow a similar plan to achieve improved investment results with higher returns, lower risk, and greater financial security. It seems like a reasonable assumption.

The six behaviors described here are not difficult to apply. It simply takes a decision to do so and the persistence to stick with it.

Remember, there are three types of people in the world. Some people make things happen; some people watch things happen; and some say, "What happened?" The rich get rich by **making** things happen—and you can too.

· POST-GAME RECAP ·

How to achieve financial independence

1. Pay yourself first.
2. Invest consistently and over the long term (time and consistency).
3. Maximize your IRA (or tax-sheltered retirement program) contribution every year using dollar cost averaging.
4. Become an owner, not a loaner.
5. Invest in solidly performing, well-managed mutual funds.
6. Learn and apply the magic of compounding.

· POST-GAME RECAP ·

How to achieve financial independence (continued)

7. Learn and use the Rule of 72 to enable your money to double as quickly as possible.

8. Pay off your mortgage.

9. Buy low-cost term insurance only.

10. Pay your credit cards off monthly.

11. Use all the tax-saving options at your disposal.

FINDING A MONEY COACH

You are forced to play the money game from the time you begin to earn a living until you die, and many of us will play it for 40, 50, 60 years or more. Don't you agree that when you're going to play a game for that length of time, it makes sense to be able to play it as well as possible? There are rules to the game, and there are strategies you can use to play more effectively and successfully.

In this game, it's important to know who your teammates are and who's the "opposition." The Internal Revenue Service of the U.S. Treasury Department makes the rules, interprets the rules, and enforces the rules of the game—the IRS is not on your "team."

To learn the rules and the strategies of the money game, you need a money coach to work with you over the long term, and more and more people are coming to this conclusion.

Coach's Quote

If you can dream it, you can do it! Do it right and do it now!

If, like many others, you are too busy to take the time to learn all the rules and strategies, or if you don't have the interest, the ability, or the inclination to learn them, then you need to find expert advice.

It's true that books like this one can provide some useful assistance, but your personal situation is unlikely to be covered in any book. You really need an individual to coach you over the long term, in all aspects of your financial life. It's my sincere belief that an experienced professional advisor can help you save thousands of dollars in taxes over time and can increase the value of your portfolio over what you can do yourself by many thousands of dollars.

Why would you not use the expertise of someone who can help you achieve those results? Well, more and more people are recognizing the advantages of seeking a money coach. But where do you look to find one?

Some people use a bank manager, but their expertise generally is limited to loans or mortgages. Accountants are often thought to be good money coaches, and no doubt many are. Again, we'd suggest you look for someone with a broader overview. Tax considerations are significant, but there are many others that need to be taken into account in creating an overall financial strategy. Lawyers are often relied upon for general financial and investment advice, but they are not trained in investment theory and may have no expertise in the area of asset allocation or in personal taxation.

I recommend you seek out someone whose professional career is completely focused on providing expert, pertinent, and timely financial advice.

WHAT QUALIFICATIONS SHOULD YOUR MONEY COACH HOLD?

Generally, someone in the field will have at least completed a securities analysis course that (along with being registered by the appropriate federal or state securities commission) allows one to sell mutual funds to the public. The securities course offered by the National Association of Securities Dealers (NASD), along with the appropriate registration, allows one to sell a full range of securities (including stocks and bonds as well as mutual funds). Stockbrokers have all completed the NASD course or an equivalent.

But those are minimum qualifications—both prerequisites for anyone registered to sell securities. You should also look for an advisor who has completed (or is enrolled in) a course leading to the Certified Financial Planner (CFP) or an equivalent designation. The CFP is offered by the Institute of Certified Financial Planners as part of its ongoing educational program. Courses are also offered by the International Association for Planning, which has no specific educational or professional requirements. Both organizations' courses cover pertinent subjects such as taxation, personal financial planning, asset management, estate planning, and so on. The American Institute of Certified Public Accountants offers a financial planning specialty designation, which may be awarded to CPAs who have met financial planning education and experience requirements.

HOW DO YOU FIND THE RIGHT ADVISOR?

Many advisors provide an ongoing series of educational seminars intended to provide up-to-the-moment information on trends in the economy, which funds are "hot," methods of tax reduction, and so on. You may find it worthwhile to attend some of these and get a sense of whether you could work with that individual.

Following are some questions you can ask a potential advisor that will help you to decide upon the money coach who's right for you.

1. What type of licensing do you hold?

   What type of products is your company licensed to sell *(e.g., mutual funds, insurance, full securities)?*

2. What is your education?

   How much experience do you have in the business?

   What credentials do you hold in the business?

3. How often will you contact me?

   Will I meet with you or a junior assistant?

   How much administrative support do you have?

4. Do you prepare a comprehensive proposal addressing my overall financial situation?

   What type of progress report will you provide? How often?

5. How are you paid?

   Are you reimbursed by the financial institutions whose products you sell?

   Do you charge a flat fee? A percentage of the value of the portfolio? A combination?

   What choices do I have?

6. What types of clients do you deal with mostly?

   Will you give me references?

7. Why should I work with you rather than someone else?

What sets you apart from other advisors?

An individual who can respond effectively and comprehensively to this barrage of questions is probably someone who can provide real value to you, your portfolio, and your entire financial situation.

Ask tough questions before you hire a coach!

• COACH'S PLAYBOOK •

How to choose your own money coach

If the services of a money coach are to be used to maximum advantage, it's important to select that coach wisely. Like any professional relationship, it will flourish if both parties remain comfortable in it, if there is trust and mutual respect, and if your confidence in the coach remains at a high level.

How then can you decide on whom you will work with? The following guidelines can help.

1. Ask friends for referrals.

If a friend whose judgment and advice you trust can offer a referral based on his or her experience, you're probably going to be happy too.

2. Ask for the names of two or three current clients.

Call these people and ask them questions about their experience with this coach. Ask whether they would recommend him or her to friends. Ask them what they like best about their coach, and finish by asking them what they like least about him or her. Their answer to that last question will tell you all you need to know.

3. Ask to see a few sample financial plans.

A reasonable plan should include information describing the current financial picture, an indication of desired future results that can be measured (complete with timelines), and a series of recommendations directly related to the desired future results. While many plans tend to go on for pages, I prefer them to be "one-page simple."

4. Choose an independent.

Some coaches are actually sales representatives for a single insurance company or group of mutual funds and can sell that insurance or those mutual funds only. Understandably, they will represent their product as being "all you'll ever need."

The fact is, however, that some mutual funds have performed better than others over the years and that some insurance companies offer lower rates than others. There are simply too many good products and companies out there to allow yourself to be restricted to the use of only one.

Work with an "independent" who represents a wide range of companies and products, and who will "shop the market" for you to offer the best products available. Within reason, I believe that a wider choice is better than a narrow choice.

5. Ask what range of services are provided.

The wider the range of services the representative provides, the easier it will be for you. Can he or she offer mutual funds, insurance, mortgage-backed securities, IRAs, Keogh plans, and annuities? Does he or she offer a mortgage-arranging service? Does he or she do income tax returns? Does he or she provide you with ongoing information updates through the use of a regular newsletter? Does he or she offer occasional large-group presentations for clients to keep them informed of changing tax law, economic conditions, etc.?

Taken together, these guidelines can help you choose the coach who's right for you.

GLOSSARY OF TERMS

Administrator (m)/administratrix (f)   The person appointed by the court to administer the estate when there is no will, or the will did not name an executor, or the named executor has died or is unwilling to act.

Alternate appointment   An alternative executor appointed in a will if the first named executor cannot or will not act.

Amortization   The process of gradually reducing a debt, such as a home mortgage.

Annuity   (1) A series of equal or nearly equal payments or receipts. (2) An agreement under which assets are turned over to an institution on the condition that the donor (or other designated person) receive regular payments for a specified period. Most often used as a retirement vehicle to provide the annuitant with a guaranteed income. *Life annuities* pay for the lifetime of the annuitant, and *annuities certain* pay for a preset number of years, whether or not the annuitant is alive to receive them. See *guaranteed term.*

Asset allocation   The relative proportions of equities, bonds, cash, real estate, and other asset types held in a portfolio at a given time. In a mutual fund, the portfolio manager often varies these proportions in an effort to maximize return when economic conditions change.

Automatic reinvestment   An option available to investors in mutual fund or other investments whereby income (dividends, interest, or capital gains) distributions are used to purchase additional units of the fund instead of being paid in cash.

Back-end load   A fee paid when the investor sells units in a mutual fund. For example, the fee might begin at 4.5% of the units' value in the first year and decline by 0.5% to 1% per year, eventually reaching 0% several years into the future. Sometimes called an *exit fee.*

Balanced portfolio   Distribution of investments into several asset categories to help increase returns and reduce risk. The basic components of a balanced portfolio are cash, bonds, U.S. equities, international equities, real estate, oil, gas, and gold. The weighting of the different components varies depending on the investor's age and aggressiveness in investing.

Beneficiary A person who receives a benefit or gift under a will, or a person for whose benefit a trust is created or to whom a life insurance policy is payable.

Bear market A stock market whose index of representative stocks, such as the Dow Jones Industrial Average, is declining in value. A "bearish" investor believes share prices will fall.

Blue chip stocks Stocks with good investment qualities. They are usually common shares of well-established companies, nationally known for the quality and wide acceptance of their products and services, that have good earning records and regular dividend payments.

Capital gain (loss) A profit (or loss) made on the sale of an asset when the market price rises above (or falls below) the purchase price (or other tax basis)—usually in real estate, stocks, bonds, or other capital assets.

Cash or deferred arrangement (CODA) Plan whereby an employee is given the option of taking cash or having an amount contributed by the employer to a 401(k) plan. In this device, contributions by the employee are treated as if they were employer contributions. There is a total annual limit of $9,500 for all retirement plans of the taxpayer (SEPs, CODAs, and SIMPLE accounts).

Certificate of deposit (CD) Evidence of a deposit, usually issued by a commercial bank or savings association. An interest-bearing investment that matures after a specified term, usually anywhere from 30 days to 10 years. The interest remains fixed during this period.

Charitable remainder annuity trust A donation strategy in which property is transferred to a trust and a charity named as the capital beneficiary. Until then, the income beneficiary can use the property and receive any income it generates. The noncharitable beneficiaries must receive an annual amount of at least 5% of the initial fair market value of all property placed in the trust.

Codicil An amendment to a will that makes changes or additions. It is executed with the same formalities as the will itself.

Common stock (shares) A class of stock that represents ownership, or equity, in a company. Common shares entitle the holder to a share in the company's profits, usually as a dividend. They also carry a voting privilege.

Compounding   Reinvesting interest as capital to earn additional interest. The frequency of compounding may be daily, weekly, monthly, quarterly, semiannually, or annually.

Compound interest   Interest earned on the amount invested, plus previously accumulated interest earnings.

Convertible term life insurance   Term life insurance that can be converted into a permanent or whole life policy without evidence of insurability, subject to time limitations.

Decreasing term life insurance   Life insurance on which the benefits are reduced yearly (or at some other interval) while the premium remains constant. In standard policies, by contrast, premiums increase and benefits remain constant.

Deferred annuity   An annuity where payments begin after the annuity is purchased—usually after a given number of years or at certain ages.

Deferred gift   A charitable donation arranged now for payment sometime in the future, often after death.

Distributions   The payments made by a mutual fund to its unit holders of the interest, dividends, and/or capital gains earned during the year. Shareholders may either take distributions in cash or reinvest them in additional shares of the fund.

Diversification   Spreading investment risk by investing in a variety of classes of assets or companies operating in different industries and/or countries.

Dividend   A portion of a company's profit paid out to common and preferred shareholders, the amount having been decided on by the company's board of directors. A dividend may be in the form of cash or additional stock. A preferred dividend is usually a fixed amount, while a common dividend may fluctuate with the earnings of the company.

Dollar cost averaging   An investment program in which contributions are made at regular intervals with specific and equal dollar amounts. This often results in a lower average cost per unit because more units are purchased when the prices are depressed than when they are high.

Earned income   For tax purposes, loosely defined as the total of income from employment and self-employment; may include pensions. Contrast *unearned income;* see also *passive activity income.*

Endowment fund   A donation made to fund a specific purpose. The charity invests the donation and uses the income generated to fund the specified project.

Equity funds Mutual funds that invest in common and preferred stock.

Estate All assets owned by an individual at the time of death. The estate includes all funds, personal effects, interests in business enterprises, titles to property, real estate and chattels, and evidence of ownership, such as stocks, bonds, and mortgages owned, and notes receivable.

Estate freeze An arrangement limiting the growth in value of the freezor's estate, by diverting the growth, usually to a subsequent generation. The purpose is to keep estate taxes to a minimum.

Exchange privilege The ability of a shareholder to transfer investments from one mutual fund to another within a "family" of funds managed by the same company. This exchange may or may not be accompanied by a transaction fee based on the asset value of the transfer.

Ex-dividend The date on which distributions that have been declared by a stock or mutual fund are deducted from total net assets. The price of the fund's shares or units will be reduced by the amount of the distribution. When you buy on or after the ex-dividend date, you do not get the dividend that was declared.

Executor (m)/executrix (f) The person(s) or institution named under a will to administer an estate in accordance with the terms of the will. If the will requires a trust to be established, rather than having the assets distributed outright to the beneficiaries, the executor/executrix will normally also be named as trustee.

Exemption equivalent trust A trust, recognized under the Internal Revenue Code, under which the spouse is entitled to all of the income for his or her lifetime, and nobody but the spouse has a right to any of the capital while the spouse is alive. Exemption equivalent trusts are most commonly created as testamentary trusts. The major benefit of an exemption equivalent trust is that the transfer of property to the trust does not trigger a capital gain and thus takes advantage of the $600,000 estate exemption for both husband and wife.

Federal Deposit Insurance Corporation (FDIC) Federal agency established in 1933 that guarantees deposits in member banks (up to $100,000) and performs other functions such as helping to prevent bank failures.

Fiduciary duty The high level of obligation assumed by a trustee. Fiduciary duty implies the highest level of care in dealing with property on behalf of a beneficiary.

Fixed-income funds   Mutual funds that invest in mortgages, bonds, or a combination of both. Mortgages and bonds are issued at a fixed rate of interest and are known as fixed-income securities.

Front-end commission charge   A sales charge based on the total value of mutual fund units purchased. The fees can range from 2% to 9% but average 4% to 5% on most purchases.

Gift in kind   A gift of property other than money.

Grantor   One who makes a grant. Also, the creator of a trust, also called the *settlor*.

Growth stock   Shares of a company whose earnings are expected to grow faster than average.

Guaranteed term   The length of time for which *annuity certain* payments are guaranteed. If the annuitant dies before the specified term, payments to the beneficiary will continue until the term ends.

Guardian   The person named to be legally responsible for the care and management of another person, for example, minor children should both parents die.

Income   The money generated on an ongoing basis through the investment of the capital (e.g., interest and dividends).

Income beneficiary   The person or persons entitled to the income generated by trust property until the time the trust is wound up. The income includes dividends and interest, but does not normally include capital gains, which form part of the capital. See also *life tenant;* contrast *remainderman.*

Income splitting   The process of diverting taxable income from an individual in a high tax bracket to one in a lower tax bracket. In many situations, married couples may reduce taxes by filing a joint tax return.

Index fund   A mutual fund designed to match the performance of a recognized group of publicly traded stocks, such as those represented by the Dow Jones Industrial Average or the Standard & Poor's 500 Index.

Individual Retirement Account (IRA)   Trust fund that individuals who receive compensation from employment (or self-employment) may establish and make contributions to. Amounts earned by the contributions are not taxed until the distributions are received. Tax-deductible contributions are generally limited to $2,000 per person, reduced in cases where an employer maintains a retirement plan. A spousal IRA may be established with up to $2,000 annual contribution for a nonworking spouse. See also *Roth IRA.*

Interest What a borrower is obliged to pay a lender for the use of a fixed sum of money.

Inter vivos trust Also known as a *living trust*, inter vivos trusts come into effect during the lifetime of the settlor.

Intestate The legal status of someone who dies without leaving a valid will.

Intestate distribution Use of a predetermined formula to distribute the estate of a person who died without a will.

Invade (capital) Many trust agreements provide for a named person to get the income for life, with the principal or capital ultimately going to somebody else. The agreement may also provide the trustee(s) with the power to pay capital from the trust to a beneficiary if certain conditions are met. The invasion power may be limited to specific needs, such as "for education" or "in case of sickness," or very broad, such as "for the general benefit" of the beneficiary.

Investment Using money for the purpose of obtaining income, capital gains, or both.

Investment fund See *mutual fund.*

Irrevocable trust A trust that cannot be revoked (canceled) by the person who created the trust (trustor, grantor, or settlor).

Issue All persons who have descended from a common ancestor. It is a broader term than "children," which is limited to one generation.

Joint and (last) survivor annuity A type of annuity that pays benefits until both the annuitant and the annuitant's spouse die.

Joint and (last) survivor insurance Coverage for two or more individuals with the death benefit payable at the death of all of the insured.

Joint tenancy A form of joint ownership resulting in the immediate transfer of ownership upon death of a joint tenant to the surviving joint owner or owners.

Leverage Using borrowed funds in an effort to maximize the rate of return on investment. A potentially dangerous strategy if the investment declines in value.

Life tenant A beneficiary who has an interest in trust property for the balance of his or her life (a life interest). For example, a trust might be set up that allows a named person to live in a house rent-free so long as he or she lives, with the house being transferred to the remainderman when the life tenant dies. Or the beneficiary may be entitled to receive all the income from the trust investments for life.

Limited partnership A partnership with at least one general partner, whose liability is unlimited, and one or more partners having limited liability.

Line of credit A flexible type of borrowing facility allowing one to borrow up to a prescribed limit and pay interest only on the amount borrowed, which may be less than the limit.

Liquidity The ease with which an asset can be sold and converted into cash at its full value.

Living trust A trust created by a settlor while he or she is alive. Also referred to as an *inter vivos trust.*

Lump sum distribution A payment from the company's pension or profit-sharing plan made to some employees on retirement. Can be "rolled" into an IRA.

Management fee The amount paid annually by a mutual fund to its managers. The typical annual fee is between 1% and 2% of the value of the fund's assets.

Marginal tax rate The rate at which tax is calculated on the next dollar of income earned. This rate increases at progressively higher income brackets.

Market timing The process of shifting from one type of investment to another with the intention of maximizing one's return as market conditions change.

MBS Mortgage-backed securities, which may provide higher yields than many other savings options. Most are invested in first mortgages on residential properties.

Money market fund Fixed-income mutual fund that invests in short-term securities (maturing within one year).

Mortgage A legal instrument given by a borrower to the lender entitling the lender to take over pledged property (usually real estate) if conditions of the loan are not met.

Mutual fund A professionally managed pool of assets, representing the contributions of many investors, that is used to purchase a portfolio of securities that meets specific investment objectives. In an open-end fund, which is the most common type, units are offered for sale by the fund on a continuous basis; the fund will also buy back units at their current price (net asset value per share). Sometimes called an *investment fund.*

Net asset value (NAV) per share (NAVPS) The total market value of all securities owned by a mutual fund, less its liabilities, divided by the number of units outstanding. When an investor in an open-end fund sells shares for cash, the price received is NAVPS.

No-load fund   A mutual fund that does not charge a fee for buying or selling its units.

Old Age, Survivors Disability, and Health Insurance   Federal government benefits paid to eligible persons under the Social Security system.

Passive activity income   Income from rental property or a business in which the investor does not materially participate. A tax loss from a passive activity generally cannot be used to offset earned income or investment income.

Personal net worth   The difference between one's assets and liabilities.

Planned giving   A charitable gift made in such a way as to maximize tax and estate planning benefits.

Portfolio   A group of securities held or owned for investment purposes by an individual or institution. An investor's portfolio may contain common and preferred stock, bonds, options, and other types of securities.

Power of attorney   A document giving signing authority for one's affairs to another person whom one trusts, to be used in one's absence or in case of inability to manage one's affairs.

Present gift   A charitable donation in which the gift is made now, not at some future point.

Probate (of will)   A judicial process whereby the will of a deceased person is presented to the proper officer or court as the last will of the testator. The court confirms the executor(s) or administrator(s) named in the will.

Probate estate   Those assets that pass through the estate and are governed by the probate document.

Prospectus   A legal document describing a new issue of securities or a mutual fund that is to be sold to the public. The prospectus must be prepared in accordance with the state or federal securities commission regulations. It must contain information on any material facts that can have an impact on the value of the investment—such as a mutual fund's investment objectives and policies, services offered, or fees charged. It must also identify any investment restrictions as well as the officers of the company.

Real after-tax rate of return   The stated rate of return, less inflation and taxes.

Remainderman   A beneficiary who is or may become entitled to the capital of a trust or estate after other interests have been satisfied.

Renewable term   A term life insurance policy that may be renewed at pre-scribed rates without evidence of insurability.

Reverse mortgage   A means of borrowing that allows a retired homeowner to use the equity built up in a home to receive a lump sum of cash and/or a monthly income.

Revocable trust   A trust that gives the settlor the power to revoke the trust.

Risk   The possibility that some or all of the money put into an investment will be lost. Also, the variability or fluctuations of an investment.

Risk-free return   The return available from securities that have no risk of loss. Short-term securities issued by the government (such as Treasury bills) normally provide a risk-free return.

Roth IRA   Contributions are not tax deductible. After a minimum 5-year holding, withdrawals are tax-free if certain conditions are met. Annual contribution limits are $2,000 for an individual having under $95,000 AGI; up to $4,000 for a married couple having under $150,000 AGI.

Rule of 72   A simple mathematical calculation used to estimate how quickly money doubles in value when interest is reinvested. In order to determine the number of years required, divide 72 by the compound rate of return. For example, at a 6% compound rate of return, it will take 12 years for money to double.

Settlor   The individual who establishes an inter vivos trust. Also called *donor, grantor,* or *trustor.*

Simplified Employee Pension (SEP)   Plan whereby an employer makes con-tributions to an employee's IRA. The maximum contribution that can be excluded from an employee's income is $30,000 (for 1996) or 15% of the employee's compensation.

SIMPLE Retirement Plan   Plan for employers who have no other retirement plan for employees and have fewer than 100 employees. A plan similar to an IRA may be established for each employee, or a cash or deferred arrangement (CODA) is allowed.

Spousal IRA   A contribution by a taxpayer to an IRA held by his or her spouse. Beginning in 1997, the maximum contribution to an IRA by a nonworking spouse is $2,000.

Tax deferral   The use of various legal methods to postpone the payment of income taxes until a later date.

Tax shelter   An investment that, by government regulation, can be made with untaxed or partly taxed dollars. The creation of tax losses in order to offset an individual's taxable income from other sources thereby reduces tax liability.

Tax sheltered retirement program (TSRP) An IRA, Keogh, 403(b), 401(k), SEP, SIMPLE, or other program that allows one to reduce taxable income by the amount invested in the program and allows tax-free income reinvestment.

Taxable income The amount of one's annual income that is used to calculate how much income tax must be paid: one's total earnings for the year minus deductions.

Tenancy in common A form of ownership in which two or more persons own the same property in equal or differing proportions. At the death of a tenant-in-common, ownership of the deceased's share transfers to that person's estate, not to the surviving tenants-in-common.

Term deposit Similar to a certificate of deposit. An interest-bearing investment to which an investor commits funds for a specified term and rate of interest.

Term insurance A form of life insurance designed to provide coverage over a specific period. It has only a death benefit; there is no savings feature or cash surrender value.

Testamentary letters A certificate confirming the authority set out in a will to administer a particular estate; issued to an executor by the court. Also called *letters testamentary*.

Testamentary trust A trust set up in a will that takes effect only after death.

Testate A person who dies having left a valid will.

Testator (m)/testatrix (f) The individual who makes a will.

Trust A legal arrangement in which one person (the grantor, trustor, or settlor) transfers legal title to a trustee (a fiduciary) to manage the property for the benefit of a person or institution (the beneficiaries).

Trustee The person or trust company that manages property according to the instructions in the trust agreement and laws governing trustees.

Trustor See *settlor*.

Total return The amount of income earned from an investment, together with its capital appreciation, expressed as a percentage of the original amount invested. It indicates an investment's performance over a stated period.

Treasury bills Short-term debt securities sold by governments, usually with maturities of three months to one year. They carry no stated interest rate but trade at a discount to their face value and mature at face value. The discount represents the return.

Unearned income Generally income from dividends, interest, and capital gains, which may be taxed differently from salaries, wages, and fees.

Unit In mutual funds, a portion, or share, of the total value of the fund. Units are purchased by investors and rise or fall proportionately with the net asset value of the fund.

Whole life A form of life insurance policy that provides a death benefit and cash value. The cash value is funded by premiums that are much higher than the actual cost of the coverage—particularly in the early years of the policy.

Will A legal document, prepared by a person in compliance with formal requirements, that takes effect on his or her death and states what he or she wants to happen to his or her property on death.

INDEX